Kierkegaard's *Fear and Tr...*

The SCM Briefly series

Briefly:
Kierkegaard's
Fear and Trembling

David Mills Daniel

scm press

The Author has asserted his right under the Copyright, Designs and
Patents Act, 1988, to be identified as the Author of this Work

The author and publisher acknowledge material reproduced from
Søren Kierkegaard, *Fear and Trembling*, ed. C. S. Evans and S. Walsh,
Cambridge: Cambridge University Press, revised edition, 2006,
ISBN 0521612692.
Reprinted by permission of the Cambridge University Press.
All rights reserved.

British Library Cataloguing in Publication data

A catalogue record for this book is available
from the British Library

978 0 334 04130 6

First published in 2007 by SCM Press
9–17 St Alban's Place,
London N1 0NX

www.scm-canterburypress.co.uk

SCM Press is a division of
SCM-Canterbury Press Ltd

Typeset by Regent Typesetting, London
Printed and bound in Great Britain by
Bookmarque Ltd, Croydon, Surrey

Contents

Contents

Introduction

The SCM *Briefly* series is designed to enable students and general readers to acquire knowledge and understanding of key texts in philosophy, philosophy of religion, theology and ethics. While the series will be especially helpful to those following university and A-level courses in philosophy, ethics and religious studies, it will in fact be of interest to anyone looking for a short guide to the ideas of a particular philosopher or theologian.

Each book in the series takes a piece of work by one philosopher and provides a summary of the original text, which adheres closely to it, and contains direct quotations from it, thus enabling the reader to follow each development in the philosopher's argument(s). Throughout the summary, there are page references to the original philosophical writing, so that the reader has ready access to the primary text. In the Introduction to each book, you will find details of the edition of the philosophical work referred to.

In *Briefly: Kierkegaard's Fear and Trembling*, we refer to Søren Kierkegaard, *Fear and Trembling*, edited by C. Stephen Evans and Sylvia Walsh, Cambridge: Cambridge University Press, 2006, ISBN 0521612692.

Each *Briefly* begins with an Introduction, followed by a chapter on the Context in which the work was written. Who was this writer? Why was this book written? With Some Issues to Consider, and some Suggestions for Further Reading, this *Briefly* aims to get anyone started in their philosophical investigation. The Detailed Summary of the philosophical work is followed by a concise chapter-by-chapter Overview and an extensive Glossary of terms.

Bold type is used in the Detailed Summary and Overview sections to indicate the first occurrence of words and phrases that appear in the Glossary. The Glossary also contains terms used elsewhere in this *Briefly* guide and other terms that readers may encounter in their study of Kierkegaard's *Fear and Trembling*.

Context

Who was Søren Kierkegaard?

Søren Abaye Kierkegaard was born in Copenhagen in 1813. His father, Michael Pedersen Kierkegaard, then 57, though successful and wealthy, was tormented by the belief that his seven children would die young, because he had once cursed the name of God. In fact, two of his children (Søren was one) survived, and Kierkegaard got on well with his father, despite the latter's unhappiness. Kierkegaard showed intellectual promise, both at school and at the University of Copenhagen, which he entered in 1830, to study theology. In the late 1830s, he fell in love with Regine Olsen, but then broke off his engagement to her, for reasons that are not clear; he seems to have gone on loving her for the rest of his life. After receiving his doctorate in 1841, Kierkegaard opted for the life of an independent scholar and writer, rather than becoming a minister in the Danish State Church, as his father had wished. His focus on the implications of religious belief and a relationship with God for the individual led him to reject the prevailing Hegelian philosophy (see Glossary) of the period, while his preoccupation with the individual, individual choice and despair mean that he is regarded as the first existentialist (see Glossary) thinker and writer. His views, and the vigorous way he expressed them, drew him into a lengthy dispute with the Danish Church, which he severely criticized for its hypocrisy and lack of religious vitality. His books include *Either/Or* (1843), *Fear and Trembling* (1843), *Philosophical Fragments* (1844), *The Sickness unto Death* (1849) and *Practice in Christianity* (1850). Due to the range of his perspectives on issues, he wrote a number of books under pseudonyms, such as Johannes Climacus and Johannes de silentio, so as to dissociate himself from the views expressed in them. He could then criticize them, and take up opposing views, if he wished. He always believed that his books would be widely studied after he died, and they have been a major influence on both theistic and non-theistic philosophers and theologians, such as Paul Tillich, Martin Buber and Jean-Paul Sartre. In 1855, Kierkegaard collapsed in the street, dying a month later.

What is *Fear and Trembling*?

Fear and Trembling appeared in 1843, and the writer is named as Johannes de silentio. Today, it is accepted that Kierkegaard's use of pseudonyms should be respected, and that it is a mistake to try to reconcile all the various elements of his thinking on theology and philosophy, found in his many writings. Below, Johannes, rather than Kierkegaard, is referred to as the author of the book.

The book (**Dialectical Lyric**) begins with a lament about the contemporary relationship of religious faith and doubt. In the past, faith has been valued, and sustaining it has been seen as a priority. But now it has become fashionable, not only to doubt, but to doubt everything. People justify their doubt by referring to Descartes, but he had not doubted just for the sake of doing so, but to find an absolutely secure base for knowledge and belief in God's existence. But what does it

2

mean to have faith? Johannes (**Tuning Up**) pictures someone, who is not a clever intellectual, but who does not wish to go beyond faith, and who has reflected on the story of Abraham all his life. He admires Abraham's total faith in God, and, whenever his own faith is tested, realizes anew how great Abraham was, and how hard it is to understand his degree of faith. He feels he would like to accompany Abraham on his journey to Mount Moriah. However, Johannes suggests a number of scenarios, in which Abraham turns out not to be a man of faith. He might doubt God's command, and try to convince Isaac that the whole episode is his own crazy idea, so Isaac will not blame God. He might doubt God's command, and become permanently depressed by the whole experience. He might be forever tortured with guilt about his willingness to sacrifice his own son. He might convey his own doubts to Isaac, and destroy Isaac's faith.

In fact, none of these scenarios occurs. On Mount Moriah (**A Tribute to Abraham**), Abraham's faith does not falter. Despite being tested so severely, he remains an exemplar of faith, as he has been throughout his life. His faith in God has taken him from the comfort of his own country, and made him a foreigner in the promised land. God has told him that he will be the forefather of many generations, and he goes on believing it, despite the fact that, realistically, he and his wife, Sarah, are far too old to have children. And then, when the long-hoped-for son arrives, God tests him again, and orders him to sacrifice Isaac. But Abraham's faith is equal to the test.

Johannes considers what faith like Abraham's means. It is not a vague hope about what may happen in the next life. It relates to this life, and to believing that, for and through God, anything, however absurd, is possible. This is why Abraham

3

can respond to God's shattering command cheerfully, confidently and trustingly without, as would be the case with somebody who lacked his faith, losing all hope for the future.

A life of faith is a demanding one, involving a willingness to make tremendous sacrifices: as Johannes puts it, 'only one who works gets bread'. The rich young man, in Jesus' parable, found it impossible to give up his money, but there is no bond of its possessor to his money, comparable to that of a father to his child. But are people consistent? They profess to admire Abraham's faith, and what he did because of it, but what if somebody, in the modern world, showed the same degree of faith, and wanted to act as Abraham did? In ethical terms, Abraham was planning to murder his son. Would not the very clergymen, who praise Abraham in their churches for the example he sets, condemn a contemporary Abraham, and want to put him in an asylum for the insane or execute him? Society would also discourage such a man for fear that foolish people might try to copy him. The nature of modern society means that faith, and what follows from it, is acceptable only if it is locked away safely in the past.

But (Johannes asks), given the preference for doubt over faith, is anyone now capable of making the movement of faith? Does anyone have the conviction of God's love necessary for making the existentialist choice for God, and plunging confidently into the absurd? Johannes imagines himself in Abraham's situation. He might do as God commands, but reluctantly, and with constant awareness of how miserable he is going to feel. Abraham, on the other hand, never doubts God and so can obey him, and then receive Isaac back joyfully. As a man of faith, Abraham goes beyond infinite resignation, which is being prepared to give up everything that matters to him in this world, in order to do what God demands of him.

He reaches faith: he knows that, with God, anything, however absurd, is possible.

Johannes conveys the difference between an attitude of infinite resignation and one of faith, through the image of two knights. The knight of faith may appear very ordinary and conventional, but everything he does reflects his belief that even the most absurd things are possible for God, and that such things can occur in this world. So, unlike the knight of infinite resignation, he does not turn aside from the world, to focus on the next. Johannes illustrates his point with a story about a young man's love for a princess, which can never come to anything. The knight of infinite resignation accepts that it is impossible, and transmutes his love of the princess into love of God, which no worldly disappointment can take away from him: but this spiritual expression of his love means he is giving up any hope of winning the princess. Not so, the knight of faith, who renounces his love, with as much difficulty as the knight of infinite resignation, but who yet believes that he will win the princess, by virtue of the absurd. He accepts that the goal is impossible, but knows that he can be saved by the absurd, taken hold of in faith. Johannes calls this the paradox of existence.

But Johannes warns his readers not to think that this 'wonderful movement' of faith is an easy one to make. While renouncing the whole world of time and space requires merely human courage, grasping it, by virtue of belief in the absurd, requires the paradoxical and humble courage of faith. Too often, faith is discussed as if it is easy, but Abraham's greatness, in being able to hold on to his faith, and go on believing in the absurd, in spite of being so severely tested, needs to be recognized, so that people today can see if they are equal to the challenge.

Do God's commands take precedence over morality? Johannes (**Problem I**) considers whether, if there is a conflict between the two, the individual who has faith should obey God's command or abide by universal ethical precepts. He poses this dilemma in the context of the moral philosophies of Kant and Hegel, in particular the latter. Kant had argued that moral laws, which must be obeyed for their own sake, and not for any other motive, or because of their consequences, and which human beings discover *a priori*, in their reason, apply universally and directly to all human beings as rational beings; and that a rational being ought never to act except in such a way that he could also will that the maxim of his action should become a universal law. However, Hegel had argued that moral laws come to be expressed in the life of a nation and its laws and customs. Instead of discovering moral laws in his own reason, the individual submits to, and complies with, his nation's universally accepted ethical precepts, and these determine his whole ethical life. As Johannes, with Hegel in mind, puts it: the individual abolishes his own individuality, to become the universal, while the ethical has no end beyond itself, but is the end of everything outside itself. However, this eliminates individual moral decision-making: such individuality is a form of moral evil. So, where does this leave a man of faith, like Abraham, who is prepared to breach a fundamental principle of accepted morality, in order to obey God's command? Either he is wrong, and should be condemned, or he is right, and the paradox of faith must be accepted: that the single individual is capable of an absolute relation with God, and is higher than universal ethical precepts, which can be set aside (teleologically suspended), to serve the higher purpose of obeying God.

To highlight his point, Johannes contrasts the suspension

of the ethical in the Abraham story with that committed by a tragic hero. Abraham's purpose is completely outside the ethical, and so he cannot be compared to, for example, Agamemnon, Jephthah or the Roman consul, Brutus, who set aside an ethical precept, in order to serve a higher ethical purpose. They were willing to sacrifice their children for reasons that lay within the ethical: the service of their nation or state. But Abraham acts for God's sake and his own: and, in doing so, breaches a fundamental ethical principle: the duty of the father to his son. Usually, the temptation people face is not to carry out an ethical duty; but Abraham's temptation, as he acts in obedience to God's command, is to do his ethical duty. But if he is wrong about God's commands, what hope is there for him? He is simply a murderer. This underlines the terrifying responsibility the man of faith assumes, when he obeys God's command, and defies society and its ethical precepts. One who subordinates his individuality to the state or society runs no risks, while the tragic hero can appeal to the outcome to justify his departure from the ethical, in pursuit of a higher ethical purpose. And society will be only too eager to give his decision retrospective approval, whatever it may have said at the time. But the man of faith, such as Abraham, must bear the full burden of responsibility for his teleological suspension of the ethical. Like Mary, the mother of Jesus, whose response to God's call was unknown to any-one else, he must be prepared to face society's castigation and condemnation.

Johannes (**Problem II**) indicates a way around the problem of a clash between duty to God and universal ethical duties: to subsume the first in the second, so that duty to God is just performance of ethical duties. This would mean that Hegel is right, and individual moral choice must be renounced, in

7

favour of obeying universally accepted ethical precepts. In which case (Johannes argues), God would just vanish into morality, and any other way of serving him would become unacceptable: so, Abraham could not be held up as an exemplar of faith. However, as there is an individual relationship to God and an absolute duty to him, the individual is higher than morality, while his relation to God determines his relation to it, not the other way round. And, if duty to God (and obedience to his commands) is absolute, it is ethical precepts which become relative, so that the knight of faith can show his love for his neighbour in ways that conflict with his duties according to morality. The paradox of the Abraham story is that, ethically, the father should love his son: he certainly should not set out to sacrifice him. But this ethical duty becomes relative, beside the absolute relation to God.

The problem the knight of faith faces is that, when someone performs an act that breaches universally accepted morality, people think he does it for his own sake, not God's. For this reason, the knight of faith cannot make himself understood by society, because he cannot express what he does in terms of society's moral code. Indeed, because he is responding to God's command as a single individual, one knight of faith cannot help another: both the greatness and the frightfulness of becoming a knight of faith is that one can do so only as a single individual. The passage from Luke's Gospel about its involving hating one's whole family brings out what absolute duty to, and love of, God demand from the individual: they must have absolute priority in his life. Not that the knight of faith stops loving others: Abraham does not stop loving Isaac. Indeed, he could not have loved him more, as he prepares to sacrifice him; but God demands him, and the duty to God is absolute. However, this duty cannot be accommodated within society's universally accepted moral code: according to it, Abraham is a murderer.

Johannes notes how society plays down the full implications of passages like the one from Luke, because it wants to encourage people to follow its ethical precepts. It wants its members to renounce individual decision-making, fearing the consequences of their doing so; and the single individual, while he retains his individuality, needs to show society that he is not a wild animal, but one who lives responsibly. Johannes reminds his readers of the loneliness of the single individual, and how much easier life would be for him, if he could abide by society's moral code, like everybody else: Abraham would prefer to be able just to love Isaac. Further, as he stands outside society's accepted moral principles and, unlike a tragic hero, has not set them aside for a higher ethical purpose, he cannot explain what he is doing to those whose lives they wholly govern. What he is doing is between himself and God: it is not within the public domain.

But what distinguishes the true knight of faith from the bogus one, or the dangerous religious fanatic? Society needs to be able to distinguish them, in order to protect itself. A noticeable characteristic of the latter is his inability to accept the true knight of faith's total isolation. He cannot bear being on his own, and being unable to explain himself to others. While the true knight of faith bears witness to his absolute duty to God, but never seeks to instruct others, the bogus one wants followers, and tries to found a sect or faction: and these are the people that society may need to defend itself against.

Johannes (**Problem III**), in a series of literary examples and illustrations, explores the question of whether Abraham is right to conceal what he plans to do from those closest to him: Sarah and Isaac. Hegelian morality demands openness. Society wants to be able to judge people's decisions, to ensure they comply with its principles; its priority is outward conformity. Further, the knight of faith could be mistaken. What he takes to be a communication from God may be a trap, laid by the devil, or the promptings of his own inadequacy or fanaticism. Sharing his experience with others would at least enable him to obtain their views about his beliefs, and test them against theirs. The trouble is that the knight of faith is acting outside morality: he cannot explain what he is doing to others, as it is something between himself and God.

Johannes adapts the traditional Danish legend of Agnes and the Merman to point up the limitations of universal morality. How does a purely ethical system accommodate the question of sin? If there is belief in God, it cannot ignore sin. Yet, if it acknowledges sin, it goes beyond itself, because sin involves the issue of individual disobedience of God and its consequences. Further, society does not recognize that some people can never comply with universal ethical precepts. In the story of Tobias and Sarah, in the Book of Tobit, Sarah shows great ethical maturity and faith in God, by believing that she can be so indebted to Tobias without hating him, and in her ability to endure pity for her misfortune. However, constant pity makes those like Shakespeare's Richard III become demonic, placing them completely outside the scope of society's so-called universal morality.

Johannes reworks the Faust legend to justify silence, as opposed to disclosure. Ethics condemns his silence, and demands acknowledgement of universal ethical precepts, but Faust is silent, in order to prevent his own doubts unsettling others. Such silence can be justified by the passage in the New Testament which tells people to anoint their heads, while fasting, so that others will not know what they are doing. But, although these illustrations highlight Abraham's inability to explain himself, there is no perfect analogy with his situation. As a character in a play, his silence could be justified, if it was to save another, but this does not apply, while ethics demands disclosure. But he cannot speak, because no one can understand his situation or the frightful responsibility that obeying God's commands involves. Instead of understanding him, if he told Sarah and Isaac, they would ask him why he could not just leave the deed. He could decide not to do it, and repent the whole thing, and then, by re-entering the sphere of morality, he could speak, and be understood; but he would no longer be Abraham. All he can do is make two movements: the infinite one of resignation, in giving up Isaac, which cannot be understood, because it is a private undertaking; and that of faith, which is his consolation, as he tells himself that God will provide a new Isaac by virtue of the absurd. He makes the infinite movement of resignation: he knows that Isaac is to be sacrificed, and that he will do it. But then he makes the move-ment of faith by virtue of the absurd: God could do something entirely different.

Johannes knows he lacks the courage to act as Abraham did. His own and subsequent ages have greatly admired Abra-ham, but no one understands him. His achievement was to be true to his love of God, and one who loves God needs nothing else: he forgets his suffering in the love. So, either there is the paradox that the single individual stands in an absolute relation to God, or Abraham is lost. Johannes (**Epilogue**) concludes with the view that no generation learns faith from previous ones: every generation has to begin from the begin-ning, and gets no further than previous ones; and the task is always sufficient for a lifetime. In each generation, many do not come close to it, and nobody goes further, while coming to it may take a long time. One who reaches faith does not come to a standstill at that point, and would be shocked if someone suggested this, for his faith will determine the whole way he leads his life.

A reading of *Fear and Trembling* reveals why Kierkegaard is regarded as the first (Christian) existentialist writer. Through the story of Abraham, Johannes de silentio sets out the choices that confront the individual: between faith and doubt; between faith and infinite resignation; and between an absolute relation with God/acceptance of an absolute duty to obey his commands and conformity to society's universal ethical precepts. The implications and costs of choosing the former are stated starkly: the knight of faith is the single individual, who must face tremendous sacrifices, total isolation, condemnation by society and the impossibility of explaining to others what he is doing. But, as a knight of faith, he knows that for God anything, however absurd, is possible and that one who loves God needs nothing else.

Johannes also explores some of the issues that surround faith, both for the knight of faith himself and for the society of which he is a member. Society is bound to be, at the very least, suspicious of the single individual, who holds that its ethical code can be teleologically suspended. Praising a knight of faith from the distant past, like Abraham, is one thing, but coming to terms with having one in its midst is another. Even if it accepts that the knight of faith is genuine, it cannot help being concerned about the impact his example may have on the impressionable and impetuous. And what about the knight of faith himself? He needs to show society that he can behave responsibly. But how can he be sure that what he takes to be a communication from God, perhaps telling him to do something that breaches a fundamental moral principle, is not a trap, set by the devil, or the promptings of his own inadequacy or fanaticism? Johannes suggests a criterion by which to distinguish a genuine knight of faith from a bogus one. The bogus knight is incapable of enduring the isolation and inability to communicate that faith in, and obedience to, God involve. He is not content just to be a witness to his own faith. He must have followers to instruct and mould. These are the people that may be a threat to society, and for whose activities it needs to watch out.

Is faith (does faith have to be) as Johannes describes it? Is it a stark choice: for God or not; for obedience to God, whatever he demands, or conformity with generally accepted morality? For many it is, and a lot of people, who have made the choice against God, have found Kierkegaard as enriching and inspiring as those who have embraced faith. For others, it is not so dramatic. Their decision may be based on evaluation of the arguments for and against God's existence, calm reflection on the meaning of life and their own experience, or a positive or negative response to religious teachings, values and practices.

Some Issues to Consider

- Kierkegaard used pseudonyms to distance himself from the contents of particular books, so that he could criticize them later, if he wished.
- It is now accepted that Kierkegaard's use of pseudonyms should be respected.
- Johannes de silentio regrets the fact that, while faith has been valued in the past, it has now become fashionable not only to doubt, but to doubt everything.

- Abraham is an exemplar of faith, but Johannes suggests scenarios in which he is not.
- Abraham goes beyond infinite resignation, which is being prepared to give up everything that matters to him in this world, in order to do what God demands.
- For those who have faith like Abraham's, it is not a vague hope in relation to the next life: it relates to this life, and means believing that, for and through God, anything, however absurd, is possible.
- Those who profess to admire Abraham's faith, when it is something in the past, may be the first to condemn someone who tries to follow his example today.
- Faith is not easy, and Abraham's greatness, in holding on to his faith, despite being so severely tested, should be acknowledged, so people today can see if they are equal to the challenge.
- If ethical precepts apply universally, Abraham, who is prepared to breach a fundamental ethical principle, in order to obey God's command, must be wrong.
- If Abraham is right, the paradox of faith, that the single individual is higher than universal ethical precepts, must be accepted.
- The story of Abraham contains a teleological suspension of the ethical: the ethical is suspended for the higher purpose of serving God.
- Abraham cannot be compared to a tragic hero, who sets aside an ethical precept, to serve a higher ethical purpose, because he acts for God's sake and his own.
- If duty to God becomes performance of ethical duties, God vanishes into morality and other ways of serving him become unacceptable.
- There is an individual relationship to God and an absolute duty to him.

- One knight of faith cannot help another, because the greatness and the frightfulness of becoming a knight of faith is that one can do so only as a single individual.
- Society prefers its members to follow its ethical precepts.
- A bogus knight of faith forms sects and factions: he cannot bear being on his own and being unable to explain himself to others.
- As the knight of faith acts outside morality, he cannot explain what he is doing to others, as it is something between himself and God.
- How does a purely ethical system accommodate the question of sin?
- Pity drives some people to become demonic, placing them completely outside society's so-called universal morality.
- If Abraham decides not to sacrifice Isaac, he will re-enter the sphere of morality, and will be able to explain himself and be understood, but he will no longer be Abraham.
- Abraham's achievement is to be true to his love of God, and one who loves God needs nothing else.
- No generation learns faith from previous ones: it must start from the beginning, and gets no further than previous ones, while the task lasts a lifetime.

Suggestions for Further Reading

Søren Kierkegaard, *Kierkegaard's Writings: Concluding Unscientific Postscript to Philosophical Fragments*, vol. 12, eds E. H. and H. V. Hong, Princeton NJ: Princeton University Press, 1992.

Søren Kierkegaard, *Either/Or: A Fragment of Life*, trans. A. Hannay, London: Penguin, 1992.

Søren Kierkegaard, *Fear and Trembling*, eds C. S. Evans and

S. Walsh, Cambridge: Cambridge University Press, 2006.

Søren Kierkegaard, *Kierkegaard's Writings: For Self-Examination/ Judge for Yourself*, vol. 21, eds H. V. and E. H. Hong, Princeton NJ: Princeton University Press, 1993.

Søren Kierkegaard, *Kierkegaard's Writings: Philosophical Fragments or a Fragment of Philosophy/Johannes Climacus*, vol. 7, eds E. H. and H. V. Hong, Princeton NJ: Princeton University Press, 1985.

Søren Kierkegaard, *Kierkegaard's Writings: Practice in Christianity*, vol. 20, eds H. V. and E. H. Hong, Princeton NJ: Princeton University Press, 1991.

Søren Kierkegaard, *Kierkegaard's Writings: Three Discourses on Imagined Occasions*, vol. 10, eds R. Gibbs and E. H. Hong, Princeton NJ: Princeton University Press, 1993.

Søren Kierkegaard, *Papers and Journals*, trans, A. Hannay, London: Penguin, 1996.

J. B. Garff and B. H. Kirmmse, *Søren Kierkegaard: A Biography*, Princeton NJ: Princeton University Press, 2004.

D. J. Gouwens, *Kierkegaard as Religious Thinker*, Cambridge: Cambridge University Press, 1996.

A. Hannay, *The Cambridge Companion to Kierkegaard*, Cambridge: Cambridge University Press, 1997.

J. Lippitt, *The Routledge Philosophy Guidebook to 'Fear and Trembling'*, London: Routledge, 2003.

W. Lowrie, *A Short Life of Kierkegaard*, Princeton NJ: Princeton University Press, 1996.

J. Watkin, *Kierkegaard*, London: Geoffrey Chapman, 1997.

Detailed Summary of Kierkegaard's
Fear and Trembling
A Dialectical Lyric
by
Johannes de silentio

Preface (pp. 3–6)

Our age is holding 'a **veritable clearance sale**' **of ideas** (p. 3). Every 'outsider and insider in **philosophy**' goes beyond just **doubting** everything, and does so 'easily' (p. 3). They say, '**Descartes** has done it', but he 'did not doubt with respect to **faith**', nor make it everyone's **duty** to doubt (pp. 3–4). A 'quiet, solitary thinker', he regarded his **method**, which was 'based partly on his **earlier distorted knowledge**', as important 'only for himself' (p. 4). Doubting, which the '**ancient Greeks**' considered a lifetime's task, is where 'everyone in our age begins' (p. 4). No one 'stops at faith'; they go further, and it would be 'foolhardy' to ask where they are going (p. 4). But, in the 'olden days', faith was 'a lifelong task' (p. 5). When 'tried and tested' oldsters drew close to the end of their lives, they could still recall 'that **fear and trembling**', which 'disciplined the youth', and which nobody entirely outgrows (p. 5). Now, 'in

17

order to go further', everyone begins where 'those **venerable** figures arrived' (p. 5).

The 'present writer' is no '**philosopher**'; he does not understand '**the System**' (p. 5). But, even if the 'whole content' of faith could be **put into 'conceptual form'**, this would not mean that it had been 'comprehended' (p. 5). The present writer is a '**freelancer**', who neither 'writes the System', nor commits himself to it (p. 5). For him, writing is 'a luxury', made more enjoyable by few people reading 'what he writes' (p. 5). He knows 'his fate' in an age when books must be written, so that they do not challenge conventional opinion, and can be quickly 'skimmed through' after dinner (p. 5). He will be 'totally ignored', or subjected to 'zealous criticism' (p. 6).

Respectfully,

Johannes de silentio

Tuning Up (pp. 7–11)

There was a man who, as a child, had heard the story of how **God** tested **Abraham**, and how he 'withstood the test, kept the faith', and then received a son, 'contrary to expectation' (p. 7). As he got older, his enthusiasm for the story grew, but he understood it 'less and less' (p. 7). He longed to accompany the sorrowful Abraham and **Isaac** on their 'three day journey' to '**Mount Moriah**', and be there when he ascended the mountain 'alone with Isaac' (p. 7). This man was 'not a thinker', and felt no need to 'go beyond faith'; rather, he thought it 'an enviable lot to possess faith' (p. 8). He was no 'learned **exegete**', and knew no Hebrew. If he had, he might 'easily have understood the story and Abraham' (p. 8).

I (pp. 8–9)

'And God tested Abraham and said to him, take Isaac, your only son, whom you love, and go to the land of Moriah and offer him there as a burnt offering upon a mountain that I will show you' (p. 8).

Abraham 'rose early', and took Isaac with him; his wife, **Sarah**, watched until they were out of sight (p. 8). After riding 'silently for three days', Abraham saw 'Mount Moriah in the distance' (p. 8). Leaving the servants, he took Isaac up the mountain. He decided he would not hide where 'this path' was taking him from Isaac (p. 8). As he blessed him, he looked 'paternal', gazed at him gently, and spoke to him encouragingly (p. 8). But Isaac did not understand. His **soul** 'could not be uplifted', and he 'begged for his young life' (p. 8). They 'climbed Mount Moriah' together, but still 'Isaac understood him not' (p. 8). Abraham turned away from Isaac and, when Isaac saw his face next, 'his eyes were wild, his appearance a fright to behold' (pp. 8–9). Abraham flung Isaac to the ground, denying he was his father, and calling himself 'an **idolater**', who was going to carry out, not 'God's command', but his own desire (p. 9). Trembling, Isaac begged God for mercy, and, as he now had no earthly father, to be his father. Abraham thanked God, because it was better that Isaac should believe that he was 'a monster' than 'lose faith' in God (p. 9).

When a child is **weaned**, the mother 'blackens her breast', so it does not look 'delightful' when the child cannot have it (p. 9). The child will think the breast has changed, but not the mother, who remains 'loving and tender' (p. 9). They are fortunate, who do not 'need more frightful measures to wean the child' (p. 9).

II (p. 9)

Rising early, Abraham embraced Sarah, the 'bride of his old age'; she kissed Isaac, who had removed 'her **disgrace**', and who was 'her hope for all generations' (p. 9). The two rode in silence. Abraham's eyes were fixed on the ground, until he looked up to see Mount Moriah. After arranging the firewood, he bound Isaac, and 'drew the knife' (p. 9). Then, he saw the '**ram** that God had chosen' (p. 9). After sacrificing it, he returned home, but could not forget God's demand of him. Although 'Isaac flourished', Abraham 'saw joy no more' (p. 9).

When a child is weaned, the mother 'covers her breast', and so the child 'no longer has a mother' (p. 9). The child is fortunate, who does not 'lose its mother in some other way' (p. 9).

III (p. 10)

Rising early, Abraham kissed Sarah, 'the young mother'; she kissed Isaac, her 'delight' and 'joy' (p. 10). Riding along '**pensively**', Abraham thought of **Hagar** and the son he had 'turned out into the desert' (p. 10). After climbing Mount Moriah, he drew the knife. Abraham rode to Mount Moriah in the 'quiet evening', and begged God's forgiveness for his willingness 'to **sacrifice** Isaac'; he had forgotten a father's 'duty' (p. 10). He rode this 'lonely trail' more than once, but found 'no peace of mind' (p. 10). He could not understand that it was 'a sin to have been willing to sacrifice to God the best he owned', and for whom he would willingly have given his own life (p. 10). If it was a sin, and he had not 'loved Isaac in this way', how could it be forgiven, as there was no 'more grievous' sin (p. 10)?

When a child is weaned, the mother, too, is sorrowful: her child will no longer be 'so close' (p. 10). They jointly 'mourn this brief sorrow' (p. 10). The one is fortunate, who 'kept the child so close and did not need to sorrow more' (p. 10).

IV (pp. 10–11)

In the early morning, everything was 'ready for the journey' (p. 10). Abraham bade farewell to Sarah. His 'faithful servant **Eliezer**' accompanied them some way along the road (p. 10). Abraham and Isaac rode 'in harmony', until they reached Mount Moriah (p. 10). Abraham prepared everything 'calmly and gently' but, as he drew the knife, Isaac saw his hand was 'clenched in **despair**'; but he still drew it (p. 10). They returned home, but Isaac had lost 'faith' (p. 11). Isaac spoke to nobody about 'what he had seen', and Abraham did not suspect 'anyone had seen it' (p. 11).

When a child is to be weaned, the mother provides 'solid food' (p. 11). The one is fortunate, who 'has this stronger nourishment handy' (p. 11).

The man thought about the story of Abraham. Whenever he 'returned home from a pilgrimage to Mount Moriah', he declared that no man was 'as great as Abraham', but who could 'understand him' (p. 11)?

A Tribute to Abraham (pp. 12–20)

If human beings had 'no **eternal consciousness**', and a 'bottomless, insatiable emptiness' underlay everything, life would just be 'despair' (p. 12). If generations just came and went, and human beings merely 'passed through the world', life would be 'hopeless' (p. 12). But, it is not so. Just as he created man and woman, God made 'the hero' and 'the poet or **orator**' (p. 12). The latter is happy, because he can admire the former, who is 'his better nature' (p. 12). He 'takes nothing for himself', but celebrates the hero in 'song and speech', so that others can also admire him (pp. 12–13). Fulfilment of 'his task' unites him with the hero, who loves him 'as faithfully',

21

for he is 'the hero's better nature': 'feeble', yet 'glorified', like a memory (p. 13). And so, no one great will ever 'be forgotten' (p. 13).

Everyone is 'great in his own way', and 'in proportion to the greatness of what *he loved*', whether it be himself or 'other persons' (p. 13). But 'the one who loved God became greater than everybody' (p. 13). Each will be remembered, but for greatness proportionate to 'the magnitude' of what they struggled with (p. 13). Struggling with the world brings the greatness of conquering it; struggling with oneself, the greatness of self-conquest; struggling with God means being 'greater than everybody' (p. 13). Conquest in the world is by power; conquest of God is by '**powerlessness**' (p. 13). Greatness can come through 'power', 'wisdom', 'hope' or 'love', but Abraham was greater than everyone, through 'that power whose strength is powerlessness'; that wisdom 'whose secret is **folly**'; that hope 'whose form is madness'; that love that is 'hatred of oneself' (pp. 13–14).

Abraham became a 'foreigner in the **promised land**', leaving behind 'worldly understanding', and taking 'faith' with him; otherwise, he would not have left his own land (p. 14). He was 'God's **chosen one**', but one 'banished from God's **grace**' would have understood his situation better (p. 14). He may have lamented his situation when sad, and to do so is human; but it is 'greater to believe' (p. 14). In faith, Abraham received the promise that all the world's generations would be blessed '**in his seed**' (p. 14). As time went by, this came to seem **preposterous**, but still Abraham believed, even though he and Sarah became 'old' (pp. 14–15). But might it have been preferable not to be God's chosen one, with all the pain it involves? Abraham might have 'wavered', and told God, without 'resentment', that he could see God's promise was not going to be fulfilled (p. 15). He would have been remembered for his example, which would 'have saved many', but he would not have become 'the **father of faith**' (p. 15). Great though it may be to relinquish a wish, it is greater still 'to keep a firm grip on it' (p. 15). Without Abraham's belief, Sarah might have 'died from sorrow'; but Abraham believed (p. 15). And it happened 'in accordance with their expectation' (p. 15) The 'wonder of faith' is that Abraham and Sarah stayed young enough to wish, and that it 'preserved their wish' and 'youth' (p. 15). There was 'rejoicing' when 'Sarah stood as a bride on their golden wedding anniversary' (p. 16).

But Abraham was 'tried once more' (p. 16). Having 'fought with time and kept the faith', God commanded him to take his beloved son, Isaac, to 'the land of Moriah', to offer him 'as a burnt offering' (p. 16). God had made 'the preposterous come true', but was now bringing it 'to nothing' (p. 16). Is there 'no compassion for this venerable old man' (p. 16)? He will be cheated of the day when, close to death, he concentrates 'his whole soul in a **blessing** that was mighty enough to make Isaac blessed all his days' (pp. 16–17). Death would now separate them, but Isaac 'would become its prey', because Abraham had laid 'a violent hand' upon him (p. 17). And it was God who thus 'tested Abraham' (p. 17).

But Abraham's faith was not the kind that led him to '**hurry out of the world to which he did not belong**' (p. 17). It was not the kind of faith that 'faintly spies its object', but is separated from it by 'a yawning abyss within which despair plays its tricks' (p. 17). Abraham 'believed precisely for this life', that he would 'grow old in the land', and then be 'forever remembered in Isaac, his dearest one in life' (p. 17). He believed, and 'he believed the preposterous' (p. 17). Had he 'doubted', he would have acted differently: which would still have been 'great and glorious' (p. 17). He would have gone to Mount Moriah; pulled out the knife; asked God not to scorn his sacrifice, even though it was not 'the best' he had; and plunged 'the knife into his own breast' (p. 17). He would have been 'admired', and remembered; but he would not be 'a **guiding star that rescues the anguished**' (pp. 17–18). Abraham believed. He asked nothing for himself, and did not 'attempt to move the Lord' (p. 18).

The Bible states that, when God called Abraham, he replied, 'cheerfully, confidently, trustingly', 'Here am I' (p. 18). He was not one of those who, in 'hard times', 'drag along the way' (p. 18). Confiding in nobody, he hurried off to Mount Moriah, as to 'a celebration' (p. 18). Many a father has found losing a child has stripped him of all 'hope for the future', but God's hand 'took it' (p. 18). Abraham's situation was worse: 'Isaac's fate' was in his hand but, although it was 'the hardest sacrifice' that could have been asked of him, he did not appeal to God (p. 18). He knew that 'no sacrifice was too hard when God demanded it', and pulled out the knife (p. 18). How was Abraham's soul 'strengthened', so that his arm did not 'limply collapse' (p. 19)? Had he doubted, had he seen the ram before he drew the knife and sacrificed it, he could have kept Isaac and gone home. But 'how changed' everything would have been (p. 19). He would have been a witness, not to 'his faith' or 'God's grace', but only to 'how frightful' going up Mount Moriah had been; it would have been remembered as the place where 'Abraham doubted' (p. 19).

'Venerable Father Abraham', you returned home having 'gained everything', and kept Isaac (p. 19). Thousands of years have gone by, but you are commemorated in 'every language' (p. 19). You are the '**second father of the human race**' (p. 19). You first bore witness to that 'prodigious passion' that '**disdains** the frightful battle with the raging elements and the forces of creation in order to struggle with God' (p. 19). Forgive any inadequacies in the way one speaks 'in praise of you' (p. 20). He will 'never forget that in a hundred and thirty years you got no further than faith' (p. 20).

Problems (pp. 21–106)

A preliminary outpouring from the heart (pp. 21–46)

The 'old adage' states that only 'one who works gets the bread', but it is not always so in the '**external world**', which operates under 'the **law of indifference**', with 'the possessor' owning everything (p. 21). In 'the **world of spirit**', where '**eternal divine order** prevails', the sun does not shine on 'both **good and evil**', and 'only the one who draws the knife gets Isaac' (p. 21). There is a '**form of knowledge**' that wants the 'law of indifference' to operate in the spiritual world, as it thinks that knowing 'the great' is enough, so 'other work' is not required (p. 22). However, it receives no bread, and starves. And what does it know? Many have heard the 'story of Abraham', but how many have been made 'sleepless' by it (p. 22)?

The story is always 'glorious', however little understood (p. 22). But how do those, who do not 'want to work', but wish to 'understand the story', speak of Abraham (p. 22)? They present the story in 'ordinary terms' (p. 22). Abraham's love for God was so great that he was willing to 'sacrifice the best to him'; but '"the best" is a vague term' (p. 22). If the '**rich young man**' **Jesus** met had sold what he had to help the poor, he would be praised for having given up the best, but, unlike Abraham, he would not have suffered 'anxiety' (p. 23). There is no '**ethical obligation**' to money, comparable to a father's '**sacred duty**' to his son (p. 23). In the story, 'the two terms, "Isaac" and "the best"' can be comfortably interchanged (p. 23). But what if someone tried to follow Abraham's example? Then, the teller of the story, in all his '**clerical dignity**', would denounce him as a '**pariah of society**' for wanting to murder his son (p. 23). Indeed, while he will have told the story of Abraham without 'warmth', he might address this 'sinner' with 'force' (p. 23). But what if the latter replies that he was only going to do what 'the **parson**' himself had urged on Sunday (p. 23). Of course, this sinner might be convinced by the 'parson's castigation', allowing the latter to return home delighted with the evidence of his own effectiveness (pp. 23–4). However, one who refused to heed the parson would end up being 'executed or sent to the madhouse' (p. 24).

So, is it just that Abraham is entitled 'to be a great man', whose deeds are always great, while those, who try to copy him, commit 'a **flagrant** sin' (p. 24)? We must think about this carefully before heaping tributes on Abraham. If faith does not make willingness to murder one's son a '**holy act**', then Abraham must be judged in the same way as anybody else (p. 24). In ethical terms, Abraham 'intended to murder Isaac'; in religious ones, to 'sacrifice' him (p. 24). Or maybe Abraham did not do what the story describes? If not, let us forget him. Certainly, if we remove faith, we are left with Abraham's intention to murder his son, which anybody without faith could imitate. It is faith that caused Abraham his 'anxiety' (p. 24). If I had to acknowledge 'as true the judgment that Abraham was a murderer', I do not know that it would silence 'my reverence for him' (p. 25). But, had that been my thought, I would have kept it to myself, as one should not share such thoughts with others.

Dare one talk of Abraham without the danger of some

26

mentally weak individual copying him? One can, even in the present age, which is not '**extravagant in faith**', as long as 'one makes faith everything' (p. 25). It is through faith, not murder, that one can acquire 'a resemblance to Abraham' (p. 25).

We can speak of Abraham, for 'the great can never do harm when construed in its greatness' (p. 25). I would start by showing that he was a 'devout and god-fearing' man, worthy of being 'God's chosen one' (p. 25). I would describe his love of Isaac, which few fathers could match. This would take 'several Sundays', but is worth giving time to, as some fathers would not wish to hear more; they would be pleased to love 'as Abraham loved' (p. 26). And, if someone, having heard of the 'frightfulness of Abraham's deed', wanted to follow the same path, I would go with him to Mount Moriah, and explain that he could withdraw from being 'tried in such a conflict', so that God would have to take Isaac, if 'he wanted to have him' (p. 26). I believe that such a person 'can become blessed', but he would be severely judged, 'even in the times of greatest faith' (p. 26).

Having 'stirred the audience', and made them aware of 'the **dialectical** struggles of faith and its gigantic passion', I would not allow them to think they had found a man of high faith, to whose 'coattails' they could cling (p. 26). I would tell them I was a 'clever fellow', who had difficulty 'making the **movement of faith**' (p. 26).

The poets honour love, but nothing is heard about faith. **Theology** just sits and courts philosophy's favour; it is said to be hard to 'understand **Hegel**', and easy to 'manage Abraham' (p. 27). Well, I understand Hegel 'fairly well', but thinking of Abraham nearly destroys me (p. 27). I am so aware of the 'prodigious **paradox**' of his life, and trying to 'get a perspective' on it paralyses me (p. 27). I can identify myself with a hero's cause, and '*think* myself *into* the hero', but not 'into Abraham' (p. 27). It is not that I think faith is 'lowly' (p. 27). It is 'the highest', and philosophy should not 'make light' of it, or 'trick people' into thinking it nothing (p. 27). I know 'the frightful', but, even if I approach it bravely, it is not with 'the courage of faith' (pp. 27–8). I find it impossible to 'plunge confidently into **the absurd**' (p. 28). I know '**God is love**', which makes me happy, but I lack the 'courage' of belief (p. 28). God's love seems '**incommensurable** with the whole of **actuality**' (p. 28). I know faith is 'higher', and that I lack its 'joy' (p. 28). Faith is convinced of God's concern 'about the least thing' (p. 28).

Can anyone now make the 'movements of faith' (p. 28)? Had I, as a '*tragic hero*' (I can go no higher), been called to Mount Moriah, I would not have skulked at home, or left the knife behind (p. 28). But I would have bemoaned my situation, and the imminent loss of all my joy. Such 'resignation' might seem 'more ideal' than 'Abraham's pettiness', but it would be a 'substitute for faith' (p. 29). I would not have loved Isaac as Abraham did, and would have 'held back' (p. 29). My conduct would have 'spoiled the whole story', putting me in 'an awkward position' when I received Isaac again (p. 29). I could not have been joyful with him, for one who cannot do more than make 'the **infinite** movement with all the infinity of his soul' only 'keeps Isaac with pain' (p. 29).

But Abraham believed, all the time, that God would not demand Isaac, while being 'willing to sacrifice him', if he did (p. 29). He believed this 'by virtue of the absurd', because there could be no 'human calculation', and it was absurd to believe that God, who had demanded Isaac, would 'revoke the demand' (p. 29). As he drew the knife, he knew God would not demand Isaac. No doubt, the outcome surprised him but, by a 'double movement', he recovered his 'original condition' and

so could receive Isaac 'joyfully' (p. 29). Had Isaac been sacrificed, he would still have believed, not in future blessedness,
but in this-worldly happiness, with God giving him another
Isaac, or restoring the sacrificed one 'to life' (p. 30). To 'lose
one's understanding and along with it the whole of **finitude**',
and then recover it through the absurd, 'appalls my soul'; but
it is 'the only miracle' (p. 30). The 'dialectic of faith' is the 'finest' (p. 30). I have a conception of it, but can only move so far
towards it. I cannot do 'the miraculous', only be 'amazed by
it' (p. 30). Abraham received Isaac back with delight, without
needing 'time to collect himself in finitude' (p. 30). He loved
God with faith, and so considered God, not 'himself' (p. 30).
He goes beyond '**infinite resignation**', and reaches faith: not
those '**caricatures of faith**' that reflect the 'wretchedness of
life', such as the '**paltry** hope' that something might not happen, because it is possible that it will not (pp. 30–1). I cannot
understand Abraham; I can only be 'amazed' by him (p. 31).
To think that one may be 'moved to believe', by reflection on
the story, is to cheat oneself, and also God, 'out of the first
movement of faith' (p. 31).

Our age will not 'stop at faith', but would it not 'be best'
to do so (p. 31)? The 'movement of faith' must 'constantly be
made by virtue of the absurd', but so that 'the finite' is not lost,
but gained 'entire' (p. 31). I can 'describe the movements of
faith', but cannot make them (p. 31). I make 'the **movements
of infinity**'; faith, after making these, makes the movements
of 'finitude' (p. 31). They are 'fortunate', who can make them;
they perform 'the miraculous' (p. 31). Unlike the '**knights of
infinite resignation**', whose 'gait is airy, bold', the 'external
appearance' of those carrying 'the treasure of faith' resembles
'**bourgeois philistinism**' (pp. 31–2).

I have not come across 'an **authentic exemplar**' (p. 32). If

Detailed summary of Fear and Trembling

I knew where to find 'a **knight of faith**', I would journey to him, to study 'how he went about making the movements' and practise them myself (p. 32). On meeting him, I would probably express surprise. I would barely be able to believe it was him, due to his resemblance to 'a **tax collector**' (p. 32). I observe him closely. Does a '**heterogeneous fraction**' of 'the infinite' manifest itself (p. 32)? Indeed not. No 'bourgeois philistine' could belong more 'entirely to the world' (p. 32). No 'heavenly look' betrays him; he is indistinguishable 'from the rest of the crowd', enjoying 'everything he sees', taking pleasure in what he eats, and generally leading a thoroughly conventional life (pp. 32–3). There is nothing of the '**incommensurability of genius** in him'; like a 'local tradesman', he lets things 'take their course' (pp. 33–4). But he does not do 'the slightest thing except by virtue of the absurd', and, 'every moment', he is 'making the **movement of infinity**' (p. 34). Although he has experienced the pain of 'renouncing' what was 'dearest' to him in the world, he can 'delight' in 'the finite' as much as one who 'never knew anything higher' (p. 34). A '**new creation**', he has 'resigned everything infinitely', and then seized it again 'by virtue of the absurd' (p. 34). Although always making 'the movement of infinity', he does so with such 'proficiency' that he 'gets finitude out of it' (p. 34). The 'knights of infinity' make 'the upward movement and drop down again' (p. 34). But, when they do so, there is a moment's hesitation, which shows they are 'really strangers in the world' (p. 34). To be able to 'transform the leap of life into a gait', and to 'express the sublime in the pedestrian', is 'the only miracle', and one only the knight of faith can perform (p. 34).

Here is an example. A young man 'falls in love with a princess'; the love dominates his life, but 'cannot possibly be realized' (pp. 34–5). The 'knight of infinite resignation', having

30

first satisfied himself his love is genuine, does not give it up (p. 35). He is willing to 'risk everything' for his love; but, seeing 'that it is an impossibility', he 'undertakes the movement' (p. 35). What will it be? He does not 'forget the whole thing'; that would be to 'contradict himself' (p. 36). He will 'remember everything', which will be painful; but, 'in the infinite resignation he is reconciled with existence' (p. 36). His love for the princess becomes 'the expression of an **eternal love**', taking on a 'religious character' and being transformed into love of 'the **eternal being**' (p. 36). So, though his love cannot be fulfilled, he is reconciled to 'the eternal consciousness of its **validity** in an eternal form that no actuality can take from him' (pp. 36–7). People foolishly talk of all things being possible for human beings. 'Spiritually speaking', perhaps; but, 'in the finite world', many things are 'not possible' (p. 37). By expressing his love spiritually, the knight of infinite resignation is 'renouncing it' (p. 37). He keeps his 'love young' within him; it needs 'no finite occasion for its growth' (p. 37). Once he 'made the movement', the princess was lost, and he takes no more interest in what she does, which shows that he has 'made the movement infinitely' (p. 37). If the princess is of a like mind, she can also join this 'order of knighthood' (p. 37). They will then be 'suited to each other for all **eternity**' (p. 38). And, if the moment ever came when their love could be 'given expression in time', they could begin 'where they would have begun if they had been united originally' (p. 38).

Infinite resignation gives 'peace and rest', and anyone, who has 'not debased himself by belittling himself', can make this movement, which 'in its pain reconciles one with existence' (p. 38). Each individual must make the movement for himself. One problem is that, these days, people have little belief 'in spirit', but it is essential to making this movement (p. 38).

And it is not easy, or instantly achievable. We would laugh at novice dancers, who thought they could immediately perform a **quadrille**, because previous generations had 'learned the positions' (p. 39). But people have this kind of attitude to the 'world of spirit' (p. 39). Infinite resignation is the 'last stage before faith', and those who have not made this movement will not have faith (p. 39). It is only in infinite resignation that 'I become **transparent** to myself in my eternal validity', and can possibly take 'hold of existence by virtue of faith' (p. 39).

What about the 'knight of faith' (p. 39)? Like the knight of infinite resignation, he gives up his love, and is 'reconciled in pain' (p. 39). But then he makes a 'more wonderful' movement, saying he believes he will win the princess 'by virtue of the absurd', and 'the fact that for God everything is possible' (p. 39). The absurd is not 'within the proper compass of the understanding' (p. 39). It is not the same as the 'improbable' or 'unforeseen' (p. 39). In the '**world of finitude**', the knight of faith's goal was impossible (p. 39). He could be saved only by the absurd, taken hold of 'by faith' (p. 40). He accepts the impossibility, but also 'believes the absurd' (p. 40).

Faith is not an '**esthetic emotion**'; it 'presupposes resignation' (p. 40). It is not 'a spontaneous inclination of the heart but the **paradox of existence**' (p. 40). The 'infinite **movement of resignation**' requires 'strength and energy and spiritual freedom' (p. 40). I see it can be done. I am amazed by the 'next movement' which, 'by virtue of the absurd', is 'to get everything'; it is 'a miracle' (p. 40). But, at the point that I wish to 'make this movement', I am seized by 'a monstrous anxiety', for 'what does it mean to tempt God' (pp. 40–1)? This is the 'movement of faith', which theology wants to sell off 'at a cheap price' (p. 41).

Faith is not needed for resignation, from which I get 'my

eternal consciousness' (p. 41). However, to go further requires faith, and this is 'the paradox' (p. 41). It is easy to confuse the movements of resignation and faith. Someone complains about losing faith, but has only reached the point where he should make the movement of resignation. Unless I am 'cowardly and soft', I can make this movement myself, and gain thereby 'my eternal consciousness in blessed harmony with my love for the eternal being' (p. 41). I renounce nothing by faith, but 'receive everything' by it (p. 41). Renouncing the 'whole of **temporality** in order to gain the eternal' demands 'purely human courage' (p. 41). To grasp 'the whole of temporality by virtue of the absurd' requires the 'paradoxical and humble courage' of faith (p. 41). Abraham did not renounce Isaac by faith, but by faith he 'received' him (p. 41). The rich young man should have given up his possessions through resignation. Then the 'knight of faith' might have told him that, if he could believe it, he would get them all back by 'virtue of the absurd' (pp. 41–2).

I can 'resign everything by my own strength', and then find 'peace and rest in the pain' (p. 42). I can 'save my soul', if I want 'love for God', rather than 'worldly happiness', to triumph in me (p. 42). But 'my own strength' will not enable me to obtain the smallest bit of 'what belongs to finitude' (p. 42). It enables me to give up the princess, and find 'joy' in my pain, but not to 'get her back', because resignation has exhausted my strength (p. 42). It is by faith, by virtue of the absurd, that I will get her. I am incapable of making 'this movement', and return to 'the pain of resignation' (p. 42). It would be 'glorious' to have the princess; the knight of faith is 'happy' and 'heir to the finite', while the knight of resignation is a 'stranger and foreigner' (pp. 42–3). To have the princess, and to live 'joyfully and happily every moment by virtue of the

absurd': that is 'miraculous' (p. 43). If all those 'in my generation', who refuse 'to stop at faith', are 'reconciled' in and by
pain, and have 'performed the miraculous and grasped the
whole of existence by virtue of the absurd', then I salute them
(p. 43). But why do people refuse to stop at faith? Why are they
ashamed to admit they have it?

Is the 'bourgeois philistinism' I see around me 'not what
it seems' (p. 44)? I am familiar with '**irony** and humor', but
they are 'essentially different from the passion of faith', and
'belong to the sphere of infinite resignation' (p. 44).

However much I want to, I cannot make 'the paradoxical
movement of faith', but everyone is capable of the 'movement
of infinite resignation' (p. 44). People must not give others
the impression that faith is 'lowly' or 'easy' (p. 44). Some people look at the Abraham story differently, interpreting it as 'a
trial', and praising 'God's grace' for returning Isaac to him
(p. 44). As a result, it becomes a 'momentary matter' (p. 45).
He will soon see the ram, and then 'the trial is over' (p. 45).
We should either 'forget Abraham', or 'learn to be horrified by
the prodigious paradox that is the meaning of his life' (p. 45).
Then we can understand that our age 'can be joyful if it has
faith' (p. 45). We must appreciate the greatness of Abraham's
achievement, so that we can decide if we have 'the **vocation** and
courage' to be tried in the same way (p. 45). We should speak
about Abraham. I would describe 'what Abraham suffered
while still believing through it all' (p. 45). His three and a half
day journey must have seemed longer than the three and a
half thousand years that 'separate me' from him (p. 45). I do
not fear 'arousing a desire in people to be tried' like Abraham,
but we must not 'peddle a cheap edition' of the story, and then
tell everybody not to do the same (pp. 45–6).

Now, I shall explore the 'dialectical factors' in the Abraham story, so that we can see the 'prodigious paradox faith is', which can turn murder into 'a holy act well pleasing to God', and restore Isaac to Abraham (p. 46). Thought cannot grasp it, because 'faith begins' where thinking 'leaves off' (p. 46).

Problem I: Is there a teleological suspension of the ethical? (pp. 46–59)

The 'ethical' is 'the universal', and applies to everybody (p. 46). There is nothing 'outside' it that is its 'telos', but it is the telos of 'everything outside itself' (p. 46). The individual has 'his telos in the universal', and his 'ethical task' is to express himself in it, abolishing his own '**particularity** in order to become the universal' (p. 46). Affirming his own particularity 'against the universal' is a **sin**, which he would have to admit to achieve reconciliation with the universal (p. 46). After entering the universal, the individual, who wishes to affirm his particularity, is in a 'state of **temptation**', and can only free himself through surrender to the universal (pp. 46–7). Thus, the ethical 'has the same character as a person's **eternal salvation**', which is 'eternally and at every moment' his telos (p. 47). It would be contradictory to say it could be 'surrendered (i.e. **teleologically suspended**)', for as soon as that is 'suspended it is forfeited' (p. 47). However, what is 'suspended is not forfeited', but 'preserved in the higher', its telos (p. 47). If we accept this, Hegel is correct to regard the qualification of human beings as particulars as a 'moral form of evil' that must be eliminated, and to hold that the individual, who remains so, 'either sins or stands in temptation' (p. 47). But Hegel is then wrong not to denounce Abraham 'as a murderer' (p. 47).

The **paradox of faith** is 'the **single individual**' being 'higher than the universal' (p. 47). Without this, Abraham and faith

35

are 'lost' (p. 47). If the 'ethical life' is 'the highest', and nothing 'incommensurable' remains in human beings, except 'that incommensurability constituting evil', the particular 'must be expressed in the universal' (p. 47). Cliché-loving people often say that 'a light shines over the **Christian world**, whereas **paganism** is shrouded in darkness' (p. 48). But, if one feels a substantial point has been said in pointing out paganism's lack of 'faith', one needs to be clear about what one means by faith (p. 48).

Faith's paradox is that the individual, as the particular, after having been 'subordinate to the universal', is higher than, and superior to, it: the 'single individual as the particular stands in an absolute relation to the **absolute**' (p. 48). This paradox is 'inaccessible to thought'; yet faith is this paradox, or it 'has never existed' and Abraham 'is lost' (p. 48). The individual may confuse this paradox with 'a temptation', but this is no reason to turn faith into 'something different', in order 'to be able to have it' (p. 49). One should admit not having it, while those who do should state 'criteria' for distinguishing 'the paradox from a temptation' (p. 49).

There is a '**teleological suspension of the ethical**' in the story of Abraham, the representative of faith (p. 49). He 'acts by virtue of the absurd', which is that he, the 'single individual', is 'higher than the universal' (p. 49). The paradox 'cannot be **mediated**' (p. 49). If Abraham does so, he admits to being 'in a state of temptation': either he does not sacrifice Isaac, or, if he does, must '**repentantly** return to the universal' (p. 49). He 'gets Isaac back again by virtue of the absurd' (p. 49). He is no 'tragic hero', but either 'a murderer or a believer' (p. 49). Abraham's ethical relationship to Isaac is that 'the father must love the son more than himself' (p. 49). Does the story contain a 'higher expression for the ethical' that can justify 'suspending

36

the ethical', without going 'beyond the teleology of the ethical'
(p. 49)?

When 'an undertaking' affecting a nation is held up 'by
heaven's disfavor', and the god 'demands a young girl as
sacrifice', people understand, as with **Agamemnon** and his
daughter, **Iphigenia**, that 'heroically', the father must make
the sacrifice (p. 50). When the 'brave **judge' Jephthah**'s vow to
God meant sacrificing his own daughter, everybody understood, for what was the point of 'Jephthah having conquered
by means of his vow if he did not keep it' (p. 50)? When a
son 'forgets his duty', and the father is responsible for carrying out the punishment, all will 'admire the father' for doing
so, as in the case of **Brutus** (p. 51). But what if Agamemnon
had sacrificed Iphigenia when there was 'a favorable wind'; if
Jephthah, on a whim, had decided to sacrifice his daughter; or
if Brutus had put to death 'a righteous son' (p. 51)?

Now what if 'these three men' had, 'at the decisive moment', asserted that it would not happen, explaining that they
believed this, by 'virtue of the absurd' (p. 51)? The difference
between 'the tragic hero and Abraham is obvious' (p. 51). The
former 'remains within the ethical', allowing the ethical to
'have its telos in a higher expression of the ethical' (p. 51).
With Agamemnon, Jephthah and Brutus, there is 'no question of a teleological suspension of the ethical' (p. 52).

But Abraham had a 'higher telos', outside the ethical, 'in
relation to which he suspended it' (p. 52). Abraham's act cannot 'be brought into relation to the universal', apart from the
fact that he 'overstepped it'; it was a 'purely private undertaking' (p. 52). The tragic hero's greatness lies in 'ethical virtue';
Abraham's in 'personal virtue' (p. 52). There is 'no higher
expression for the ethical in Abraham's life than this, that the
father must love the son' (p. 52). However, Abraham acts as

he does for God's and 'his own sake': because God demands 'proof of his faith', and so he can prove his faith (p. 52). This is 'a trial, a temptation', but temptation usually distracts a person from 'his duty' (p. 52). With Abraham, 'the temptation is the ethical itself', which would have prevented him carrying out **God's will** (p. 52). What is 'the duty' (p. 52)? It is 'precisely the expression for God's will' (p. 52).

We need 'a new category' for Abraham (p. 52). The tragic hero does not have a 'private relation' with the divine: **the 'ethical is the divine'**, so 'the paradox in it can be mediated in the universal' (p. 52). Abraham 'cannot be mediated': to speak, he would have to 'express himself in the universal', which would mean describing his situation as 'a temptation' (pp. 52–3). There is 'no higher expression for the universal that ranks above the universal he oversteps' (p. 53). So, what do we make of Abraham, who 'gives up the universal', to 'grasp something still higher' (p. 53)? If he is mistaken, or has 'misunderstood' God, 'what salvation is there for him' (p. 53)? Will he not have destroyed 'his joy in the world' (p. 53)? The tragic hero performs his exploit at a certain point in time, but is forever able to make others forget their 'sufferings' in his (p. 53). Abraham is different. One approaches him with 'religious awe', trembling 'with anxiety', aware of the possibility that he may be wrong (p. 53). Even Shakespeare, 'who can say everything', did not describe 'this torment' (p. 54).

If 'the ethical' is thus 'teleologically suspended', how does the 'individual in whom it is suspended exist' (p. 54)? As 'the particular in contrast to the universal', does he sin (p. 54)? This is 'the **form of sin**', and, if it cannot 'be repeated' in a way that 'it is not sin', judgement falls on Abraham (p. 54). Abraham existed by believing. The 'paradox', which he cannot explain to anyone else, is that, as the 'single individual', he puts himself 'in an absolute relation to the absolute'; if he 'is justified', it is by being 'the particular', not 'something universal' (p. 54).

How can the individual be certain 'he is justified' (p. 54)? **Reducing 'all existence' to 'the idea of the state', or 'society'**, makes it easy 'to mediate', because one does not encounter the paradox that the individual, as the particular, is 'higher than the universal' (p. 54). If a hero offends society, by becoming a paradox it does not understand, he may argue that he will be justified in 'the outcome' (p. 55). In our age, which 'does not produce heroes', such words are spoken by **associate professors** who, holding secure positions in a **well-organized state**, arrogantly presume to 'judge the great men' (p. 55). They do not realize that it is 'the beginning' to which one should pay attention (p. 55). The hero only knows that the outcome is splendid when his deed is 'over': further, it is 'in its dialectic altogether heterogeneous to the hero's existence' (p. 55). Did his getting Isaac 'by a *miracle*' justify Abraham in relating himself 'as the single individual to the universal' (pp. 55–6)? Would he have been 'less justified', if he had sacrificed Isaac (p. 56)? Yet, people are eager to know the outcome, rather than 'the anxiety, the distress, the paradox' (p. 56). Although it is like 'a prize in the lottery', they feel 'edified' when they have heard it (p. 56).

'What I do', not 'what happens to me', makes me great (p. 56). No one should think a person great, because he was prize-winner in a 'lottery' (p. 56). What helps to make us great is 'the anxiety and distress in which the great are tried' (pp. 56–7). What we wish to make great, through 'empty and hollow phrases', we will destroy (p. 57). Nobody in the world was greater than 'the mother of God, the **Virgin Mary**', but she was not made great just by being '**favored among**

women' (p. 57). What is omitted is 'the distress, the anxiety, the paradox' (p. 57). The angel did not visit other women in Israel, to tell them not to despise Mary, because 'something extraordinary' was 'happening to her' (p. 57). So, nobody understood her. She is great because she was content to be God's **'handmaid'** and, just as Abraham did not require 'tears', she demanded 'no worldly admiration' (p. 57). Both 'became greater' through their 'distress and torment' (p. 57). It may be good that the poet invites us to 'weep' for the tragic hero, because 'he deserves it'; but it is better that the 'knight of faith' tells the weeping person to weep, not for him, but for himself (p. 58). We think it would have been wonderful to have seen 'Christ walking about in the promised land' (p. 58). But it is easy to forget 'the anxiety, the distress, the paradox' (p. 58)! Was it so easy to become 'an **apostle**' then (p. 58)? Of course, after 'eighteen centuries', given the outcome, it seems straightforward (p. 58). It assists the 'paltry deception whereby one deceives oneself and others' (p. 58).

As for Abraham, before 'the outcome', either he was a murderer, or 'we are at the paradox that is higher than all mediations' (p. 58). His story contains 'a teleological suspension of the ethical' (p. 58). A 'single individual', he rose higher 'than the universal' (p. 58). This is the 'paradox that cannot be mediated' (p. 58). Otherwise, he is a mere murderer. One can become a 'tragic hero' through one's 'own strength', but not a 'knight of faith' (p. 58). Faith is 'a miracle' from which none is 'excluded' (p. 59). It is 'a passion', and passion 'unites all human life' (p. 59).

Problems (pp. 21–106)

Problem II: Is there an absolute duty to God? (pp. 59–71)

The 'ethical is the universal', and so is 'the divine'; thus, every duty is 'duty to God' (p. 59). But this means there is 'no duty to God', as duty does not involve a 'relation to God' (p. 59). Talk of 'duty to love God' is **tautologica**l, because 'God' stands for 'duty', and so becomes 'an invisible vanishing point', with only ethical 'power'; and this makes wanting to love God, in some other way, look 'suspicious' (pp. 59–60). If 'there is nothing incommensurable in human life', except what is there accidentally, Hegel 'is right'; but then Abraham cannot be faith's 'father' (p. 60). For Hegel, the 'outer' is 'higher than the inner', but the paradox of faith is that it is the other way around (p. 60). The 'ethical view of life' requires the individual to remove 'the qualification of inwardness', and express it in 'outward form'; so, the individual who wants to hold on to 'the inward qualification of feeling' 'stands in temptation' (p. 60). But, faith involves a 'new inwardness', which is 'incommensurable with the outer' (p. 60). 'Recent philosophy' lumps faith with 'feeling, mood' and so on, but faith is 'preceded by a movement of infinity'; it begins 'unexpectedly', by 'virtue of the absurd' (pp. 60–1). If faith is only what philosophy claims it is, **Socrates** went further than it, instead of not reaching it. It is only when the individual has 'exhausted himself in the infinite' that faith can 'break forth' (p. 61).

Faith's paradox is the individual being 'higher than the universal', determining his relation to it by 'his relation to the absolute', not vice versa (p. 61). This also means there is 'an absolute duty to God', in which the individual 'relates himself... absolutely to the absolute' (p. 61). And, if 'duty' to God is absolute, the ethical becomes 'relative', and its expression 'paradoxical', such that loving God can lead the 'knight of faith' to love his neighbour in ways 'opposite' to 'what duty is ethically' (p. 61). However, once the individual wants to 'express his absolute duty in the universal', he considers himself 'in a temptation' (p. 61).

Thus, we have the 'paradox' of the Abraham story (p. 62). Ethically, 'the father must love the son', but this 'ethical relation' becomes 'relative', when set against 'the absolute relation to God' (p. 62). When someone performs an act that 'does not conform to the universal', one thinks he does it, for his own, not 'God's sake' (p. 62). So, it is both 'the highest **egoism**' and 'the most absolute devotion' to God (p. 62). If faith is 'mediated into the universal', it is '**annulled**' (p. 62). Because of this paradox, the 'single individual' cannot 'make himself intelligible to anyone' (p. 62). And, as 'partnership' is 'unthinkable', 'one knight of faith' cannot help another; either the individual becomes one by 'assuming the paradox' or he never does (p. 62). If one could decide, in general terms, 'what is to be understood by Isaac', the individual could not 'convince' himself of it through others, but 'only by himself as the single individual' (pp. 62–3). The 'greatness' and the 'frightfulness' of becoming a knight of faith is that one can only do so as 'the single individual' (p. 63).

Luke 14.26 contains a 'hard saying' about 'absolute duty to God': one must hate one's whole family to be Jesus' '**disciple**' (p. 63). Scholars water this down, by interpreting 'hate' as to 'love less'; but the words 'must be understood literally' (pp. 63–4). One should appreciate the 'greatness' of these words, even if one lacks 'the courage to do that oneself': God 'demands absolute love' (p. 64). What does talk of 'hate' mean here (p. 64)? It can only be understood as a paradox. The 'absolute duty' to God may lead one to do what '**ethics**' would forbid', but cannot make 'the knight of faith stop loving' (p. 65). At the point that Abraham is prepared to sacrifice Isaac, the 'ethical expression' for it is that he hates him (p. 65). But, as 'God demands Isaac, Abraham must love him, if possible, even more dearly, and only then can he *sacrifice* him' (p. 65). It is his 'love for Isaac' that, in 'paradoxical opposition to his love for God makes his act a sacrifice' (p. 65). His 'distress and anxiety' in the paradox preclude his making himself understood, but he only sacrifices Isaac when 'his act is in absolute **contradiction** to his feeling' (p. 65). But 'the reality of his act is that by which he belongs to the universal', and there he is 'a murderer' (p. 65).

The knight of faith cannot justify his action by a 'higher expression of the universal (as the ethical)': his sacrifice is not for the sake of his church, which '**qualitatively**' resembles 'the state' (p. 65). An '**ecclesiastical hero**' expresses 'the universal' in his actions, and will be understood; but he is not a knight of faith (p. 65). Fear of the consequences of individuals behaving as individuals accounts for the reluctance to draw attention to passages like the one from Luke; the prevailing view is that people should be forced 'into becoming the universal' (p. 65). One who realizes how 'terrifying' living as an individual is, will also say it is 'the greatest': though, this must not be said so as to lay 'a trap for someone gone astray', but in a way that assists him 'into the universal' (pp. 65–6). Fearing to mention such passages is to fear mentioning Abraham. One concerned for his soul believes that to live 'in the world', under one's own 'supervision', is to live 'strictly' (p. 66). One must show one is not 'a wild animal', in need of 'coercion', by speaking 'with fear and trembling' (p. 66).

While 'the tragic hero resigns himself in order to express the universal', the knight of faith 'resigns the universal in order to become the single individual' (p. 66). Far from finding this easy, he is only too conscious of the glory of belonging to the universal; of being 'intelligible' to himself 'in the universal';

and of having others understand it 'through him' (p. 66). He knows, too, the 'lonely trail, narrow and steep', and the frightfulness of being 'outside the universal' (p. 66). He is 'mad' to pursue it, but he is either that or 'a **hypocrite**' (p. 67).

Abraham may well have wished his 'task' was simply to love Isaac, 'as a father would and should', and that any sacrifice of him was 'for the universal', to 'inspire' other fathers (p. 67). But he knows he is being 'tried and tested' himself, and can do 'nothing for the universal' (p. 67). What can we say of Abraham in human terms? It takes him 'seventy years to get a son', then he 'wants to sacrifice him' (pp. 67–8). He must be mad. And Abraham could not 'explain' it further; his life is '**under divine injunction**', and not in the '**public domain**' (p. 68). But there is the 'wondrous glory' the knight achieves in 'becoming **God's confidant**', and calling him 'You' in heaven (p. 68). However, while the tragic hero can be 'secure in the universal', the knight is 'constantly' tried, 'kept sleepless', and tempted by awareness that he can 'return repentantly to the universal' (p. 68).

The knight of faith has 'the passion to concentrate in a single moment the whole of the ethical he **violates** in order to give himself the assurance that he actually loves Isaac' (p. 68). The tragic hero, although he 'concentrates in one moment **the ethical he has transcended teleologically**', has a place of refuge in 'the universal'; but the knight of faith is 'alone in everything' (p. 69). Abraham, unlike Agamemnon, has no 'place of resort' in the universal (p. 69). However, he makes 'one more movement', concentrating his soul 'back upon the miracle' (p. 69). Without that, he is just like Agamemnon: as long as he can justify willingness to sacrifice Isaac when he does not thereby 'benefit the universal' (p. 69).

Only the individual can decide whether he is a knight of

faith, or just 'in a state of temptation', but the former has a possible 'distinguishing characteristic' (p. 69). While the 'true knight of faith' is in 'absolute isolation', the false one 'is **sectarian**'; he cannot bear the 'frightfulness' of being 'only the single individual' (pp. 69–70). The false knight, a 'sectarian weakling', ignorant of the 'lonely spiritual trials' the true knight must undergo, joins with others (p. 70). The true knight, while feeling 'the pain' of being unable to 'make himself intelligible' to others, has no wish 'to instruct' them (p. 70). The false knight does not realize that an individual cannot become a 'single individual' as a result of another's 'guidance', and that a true knight is '**a witness, never a teacher**'; and so he is eager to share his 'acquired proficiency' with others (p. 70). The true knight knows he did not 'gain what he gained on the cheap', so does not 'sell it on the cheap' (pp. 70–1). Therefore, either there is 'an absolute duty to God', and this is the paradox that 'the single individual stands in an absolute relation to the absolute', or faith has 'never existed' and 'Abraham is lost' (p. 71).

Problem III: Was it ethically defensible of Abraham to conceal his undertaking from Sarah, from Eliezer, from Isaac? (pp. 71–106)

The 'ethical' is the 'universal' and the 'disclosed', whereas the 'single individual' is 'the concealed', whose responsibility is to 'become disclosed in the universal' (p. 71). Unless 'the single individual as the particular' can be 'higher than the universal', Abraham's behaviour cannot be defended (p. 71). Hegel's philosophy admits of 'no justified concealment', and requires 'disclosure'; but it is then inconsistent in considering Abraham to be 'the father of faith' (p. 71). Let us examine the question 'purely esthetically', in the category of 'the *interesting*', which is on the 'boundary between **esthetics** and ethics' (p. 72).

In drama, wherever 'recognition' can be mentioned, a 'prior concealment is implied' (p. 73). Recognition is the 'relaxing element in the dramatic life'; concealment 'is the element of tension' (p. 73). But, as modern drama has dispensed with 'the **idea of fate**', concealment and disclosure are 'the hero's free act for which he is responsible' (p. 73). My job now 'is to carry concealment dialectically through esthetics and ethics', so that 'esthetic concealment and the paradox appear in their absolute dissimilarity' (p. 74). Imagine two young people, 'secretly in love', who have not told each other (p. 74). The girl's parents want to coerce her into marrying someone else. Now, these two are '**responsible esthetically**' for choosing to conceal their love (p. 75). However, esthetics is a '**sentimental discipline**', so 'a coincidence' reveals their true feelings, and they 'get each other and also a place among real heroes' (p. 75). Ethics, on the other hand, disdains sentimentality and coincidence. It 'denounces as presumptuous' the hero's desire to '**play providence**', and to do so 'by his suffering'; and deplores existence of 'a secret they have assumed on their own responsibility' (p. 75). Thus, 'esthetics demanded concealment and rewarded it; ethics demanded disclosure and punished concealment' (p. 75). For ethics, the hero may believe his silence makes 'it easier for others', but it may also make it easier for him (p. 76). By his silence, 'the tragic hero' takes on 'a responsibility as the single individual', while ethics requires that 'he constantly expresses the universal' (p. 76). Yet, 'secrecy and silence', as '**qualifications of inwardness**', can 'make for greatness in a person' (p. 77). But, 'I always stumble upon the paradox, the divine and the **demonic**' (p. 77). Silence is 'both of these': the 'demon's snare' and the '**deity's communion** with the single individual' (p. 77).

Before going back to Abraham, I shall discuss 'a few poetic personages', whose 'anxiety' may bring something 'to light' (p. 77). **Aristotle** has a story of a man who, having been told at **Delphi** that marriage will bring him 'misfortune', decides not to marry (pp. 77–8). The actual incident 'hardly came off without tears', but let us consider this bridegroom, whom the 'divine pronouncement' has made 'as unhappy as the bride', and his possible courses of action (pp. 78–9). He could say nothing, marry, and hope for the best, comforting himself with the thought that he will have maintained his 'love' and that misfortune was foretold only 'for *him*' (p. 79). But he would have to take 'responsibility' for his silence and his wife's 'righteous indignation' at it (p. 79). He could say nothing and not marry, but would destroy 'himself in his relation to her'; such behaviour would be offensive to 'the girl and the reality of her love' (pp. 79–80). He might speak out. However, as only he faces misfortune, he and his intended bride lack 'a **common expression for their suffering**'; they cannot 'decide jointly to defy heaven together with its misfortune' (p. 80).

Now, ethics would 'require him to speak'; and this story, in which I do not get beyond 'the tragic hero', does 'cast light on the paradox' (pp. 80–1). In ancient Greece, the '**augur's pronouncement**' of misfortune would have been generally 'intelligible' (p. 81). So, if the hero wishes to speak, he will be understood. If he chooses silence, it is because, as 'the single individual he wants to be higher than the universal', and 'delude himself' with 'fantastic notions' about how his intended bride will 'forget this sorrow' (p. 81). But, if he had obtained this knowledge 'quite privately', he 'could not speak', however much he wished to do so; he would then be silent, not because, as a single individual, he wanted to place himself 'in an absolute relation to the *universal*', but because he had been 'placed as the single individual in an absolute relation to the *absolute*' (pp. 81–2).

As an example, 'along the lines of the demonic', I shall take 'the **legend of *Agnes and the Merman***', in which the latter is 'a seducer', who bursts from the depths, and 'in wild lust grabs and breaks the innocent flower' (p. 82). But let us imagine Agnes feels the merman is 'what she was seeking' (p. 82). About to plunge into the sea 'with his prey', he sees her look of complete belief and humility, as she 'entrusts her entire destiny to him' (pp. 82–3). Unable to 'withstand the power of innocence', he takes Agnes 'home again', returning alone to the raging sea and his own 'despair' (p. 83).

We shall now give the merman 'a **human consciousness**'; his being a merman will 'denote a **human pre-existence** in whose consequences his life was **ensnared**' (p. 84). He can become 'a hero'; he has been 'saved by Agnes, the seducer is crushed' (p. 84). But 'two forces contend for him': 'repentance' and 'Agnes and repentance' (p. 84). The first means conceal-ment, the second disclosure. If he stays concealed, he makes 'Agnes unhappy', for she 'loved him in all her innocence' (p. 84). The merman himself will also be unhappy, and the 'demonic element in repentance' will 'explain to him that this is precisely his punishment' (p. 84).

By abandoning himself 'to this demonic element', he could 'then make another attempt to save Agnes' (p. 84). He knows she loves him; if he could tear 'this love' from her, 'she would be saved' (p. 84). But how should he do this? He does not think she will be disgusted by a 'candid confession' (p. 84). He could 'mock her', 'hold her love up to ridicule', and thus 'provoke her pride', sparing 'himself no anguish' in the process (p. 84).

Through 'the demonic', which is like 'the divine', in that 'the single individual can enter into an absolute relation to it', the merman 'would be the single individual who as the particular was higher than the universal' (p. 85). This is 'the **analogy**, the counter-part to that paradox of which we speak' (p. 85). While the merman seems to have evidence that his 'silence is justified', as he 'suffers all his pain in it', he can speak, and become 'a grand tragic hero' by doing so (p. 85). He 'stands at a dialectical **apex**' (p. 85). If he is rescued 'out of the demonic in repentance', 'two paths' are open to him (p. 85). If he remains 'in concealment', he will not 'come as the single individual into an absolute relation to the demonic', but will fall back on 'the **counter-paradox** ' that 'the divine will save Agnes' (p. 85). Or 'he can be saved by Agnes', in that 'he is saved insofar as he becomes disclosed' (p. 86). But he must 'have recourse to the paradox' (p. 86). When the 'individual' has, 'by his guilt', 'come outside the universal', he can 'only return to it', by 'having come as the single individual into an absolute relation to the absolute' (p. 86). Sin is not 'the first **immediacy**', but a later one (p. 86). In sin, the 'individual is already higher, in the direction of the demonic paradox, than the universal', as 'it is a contradiction for the universal to want to require itself of one who lacks the **necessary condition**' (p. 86). An ethics that 'ignores sin' is 'an altogether futile discipline' but, if it 'asserts sin', it is, 'for that very reason beyond itself' (p. 86). Philosophy teaches that 'the immediate should be annulled' but, while that 'is true', it is not the case that 'sin, any more than faith, is the immediate as a matter of course' (p. 86).

All this does not explain Abraham, who did not 'become the single individual through sin', but was a 'righteous man', God's 'chosen' (p. 86). The 'analogy to Abraham' will only be clear 'after the single individual is brought to a position of being able to perform the universal' (p. 86). I can understand the 'merman's movements', but not Abraham's (p. 86). It is 'through the paradox' that the merman 'comes to want to realize the universal' (p. 86). If he 'remains concealed', and is 'initiated into all the agonies of repentance', he becomes 'demoniac', and 'is destroyed' (pp. 86–7). If he remains concealed, but does not 'shrewdly think' that, by 'being tormented in the bondage of repentance he can work Agnes loose', he will find 'peace but is lost to this world' (p. 87). But, if he 'becomes disclosed and lets himself be saved by Agnes', he is 'the greatest person I can imagine' (p. 87). He cannot belong to Agnes unless, after the 'infinite movement of repentance', he makes 'the movement by virtue of the absurd' (p. 87). One with insufficient 'passion' to make either movement can easily believe he has achieved 'the highest', and can help others do so, because he can persuade himself that the 'world of spirit' is like 'a card game where everything happens by chance' (p. 87). Yet, if this really is an age in which the highest is commonly achieved, why is 'doubt about the **immortality of the soul**' so general (p. 87)? One who 'has made merely the movement of infinity scarcely doubts' (p. 87). Entering a monastery may not be life's 'highest' course, but I do not consider that, these days, when nobody does, we are all 'greater than the deep and earnest souls', who did (pp. 87–8). How many people, today, have sufficient 'passion' to 'think this and then to judge themselves honestly' (p. 88)? But what 'higher movement' have we pursued, since we stopped 'entering the monastery' (p. 88)? Have we not developed a form of 'worldly wisdom', which deceives us into believing we have 'attained the highest', and thus stops us 'even attempting lesser things' (p. 88). Only one movement remains after the 'monastic': that of 'the absurd' (p. 88). But how many people today 'understand what the absurd is' (p. 88)? Our age ceaselessly 'demands the **comic**'; what it actually requires is 'courage to believe in the power of the spirit', and to stop 'cravenly stifling its better impulses and enviously stifling them in others' (p. 89). It needs 'an enthusiastic figure' to remind it of 'what was forgotten' (p. 89).

The '**Book of Tobit**' contains a 'touching' story (p. 89). **Tobias**, an only child, wants to marry Sarah, who has been married 'to seven men', who all 'perished in the bridal chamber' (p. 89). I shall change this, to remove any 'comic effect' (p. 89). Sarah has 'never been in love', but wants 'to love a man with her whole heart' (p. 89). However, she is intensely unhappy, as she knows that an 'evil demon' will 'kill the bridegroom on the wedding night' (p. 89). This made Sarah particularly unfortunate: it is 'hard not to find the person to whom one can give oneself, but it is *unspeakably* hard not to be able to give oneself' (p. 90). Just imagine the fear that overshadowed the wedding preparations and ceremonies. But when they were 'shut up together', Tobias said to Sarah that they should pray together for God's 'mercy' (p. 90).

Now, if a poet made use of this story, he would focus on Tobias' 'heroic courage' in thus risking his life (pp. 90–1). But 'Sarah is a heroine' (p. 91). Look at the '**ethical maturity**' she shows in allowing 'the beloved' to undertake 'such a daring venture' on her behalf (p. 91). What 'humility' she shows 'before another human being', and 'faith in God that the next moment she would not hate the man to whom she owed everything' (p. 91). Imagine a man in her position, and 'the demoniac is immediately at hand' (p. 91). A 'proud, noble nature' can endure anything, including punishment for sin; but 'it cannot tolerate' pity (p. 91). And Sarah is destined to be 'tormented by human pity'; to think of her is to say, 'The poor girl' (p. 91). Look at Shakespeare's **Gloucester** in *Richard III*.

What 'made him a demoniac' was 'his inability to bear the pity' he was shown 'from childhood on'; 'natures like Gloucester's cannot be saved by mediating them into an idea of society', because ethics 'only makes a fool of them' (pp. 92–3). It would be like chiding Sarah for not expressing 'the universal' and marrying (p. 93). People like Gloucester are simply '**placed outside the universal by nature or historical circumstance**' (p. 93). They are not 'personally to blame' for it, but it is 'the beginning of the demonic' in them (p. 93).

The '**legend of *Faust***' is another example of 'an individual wanting to save the universal by his concealment and silence' (p. 94). Faust is 'the doubter par excellence'; he knows the spirit 'sustains existence', but that the majority's 'security and joy' is based on '**unreflective happiness**' (p. 95). He knows what he could 'do with his doubt': 'frighten people into being terror-stricken' (p. 96). But he has 'a sympathetic nature', and 'keeps silent', hiding his doubt, and doing his best 'to walk in step with other people'; he 'makes himself a sacrifice to the universal' (p. 96).

The doubter 'hungers just as much for the **daily bread of life** as for the nourishment of the spirit' (p. 96). He 'sees **Margaret**' and, as 'my Faust does not choose lust at all', while 'his soul has preserved love for humankind', he can 'well fall in love with her' (p. 96). However, 'true to his resolve', he tells no one of his doubt, nor 'Margaret of his love' (p. 97). He is 'too ideal a figure' to convince himself that, by speaking, he would 'bring about a general discussion', or that doing so could 'come off without consequence' (p. 97). He is silent 'to sacrifice himself', as he knows that speaking will 'put everything into disorder' (p. 97). Ethics 'condemns' his silence, demanding acknowledgement of 'the universal'; and one should remember this when censuring 'a doubter' for speaking out

(p. 97). If a doubter, 'on his own responsibility', says nothing, 'the universal will constantly torment him', accusing him of acting from 'hidden pride' (p. 98). But, if he can 'become the single individual who as the particular stands in an absolute relation to the absolute', he can obtain 'authorization' for his silence (p. 98). He 'must turn his doubt into guilt', and so 'is in the paradox'; but, 'if so, his doubt is cured, even though he may acquire another doubt' (p. 98).

The New Testament accepts 'such a silence'; it contains passages that 'commend irony, provided it is used to conceal something better' (p. 98). But, these days, people do not wish to know more about irony than 'has been said by Hegel', who did not understand or approve of it (p. 98). In the **Sermon on the Mount**, we are told that, when fasting, we should anoint our heads and wash our faces, so that others will not notice we are fasting. This passage affirms that '**subjectivity** is incommensurable with actuality, even that it has a right to deceive' (p. 98).

How did Abraham act? The point of the 'investigation' above was to highlight his 'unintelligibility' (p. 99). There is no 'analogy' that helps to 'explain Abraham' (p. 99). He did not speak 'to Sarah, to Eliezer, or to Isaac', the three 'ethical **agents**'; and, for Abraham, there was 'no higher expression' of the ethical than 'family life' (p. 99).

'Esthetics' would permit the 'single individual' to keep silent to 'save another' (p. 99). But Abraham's silence is not for Isaac's sake. He is sacrificing him 'for his own sake and for God's', and thus offends against esthetics, which can accommodate sacrifice of self, and silence about it, but not sacrifice of another for one's own sake (p. 99). Ethics, however, 'demands disclosure' (p. 99). The 'genuine tragic hero' sacrifices himself 'for the universal', and is 'open' about it (p. 99).

So, here is the paradox: either the 'single individual' can have 'an absolute relation to the absolute', meaning ethics is 'not the highest', or Abraham, neither a tragic, nor an 'esthetic', hero, 'is lost' (p. 99).

Abraham '*cannot* speak', wherein is his 'distress and anxiety' (p. 100). Speaking 'translates' one 'into the universal' (p. 100). Abraham can talk of his love for Isaac, but not of his willingness to 'sacrifice Isaac' (p. 100). Nobody can understand this, his 'trial' (p. 100). This is where he differs from the tragic hero, who is unfamiliar with 'the frightful responsibility of **solitude**' (p. 101). He would like to give 'a blessed consolation for the whole world', but cannot do so, for Sarah, Eliezer and Isaac would ask him why he was going to do this deed, and why he could not just leave it (p. 101). He cannot speak, because 'he speaks in a **divine** language' (p. 101). He could stop at any moment, and 'repent the whole thing as a temptation' (p. 101). Then, he could speak, and be understood; but he would no longer be Abraham.

Abraham cannot explain that his 'trial' is one where '**the ethical is the temptation**', and so he is an '**emigrant** from **the sphere of the universal**' (p. 101). Abraham 'makes two movements': the 'infinite movement of resignation', in giving up Isaac, which cannot be understood, because it is 'a private undertaking', and 'the movement of faith' (p. 101). The latter is 'his consolation', as he tells himself that God will provide 'a new Isaac, namely by virtue of the absurd' (p. 101). Only Abraham's reply to Isaac 'has been preserved': that God would 'provide the lamb for the burnt offering' (p. 102). I shall consider this 'in more detail' (p. 102). Is it appropriate for a tragic hero to make 'a final remark' (p. 102)? Not if the 'significance of his life' lies in an 'external deed'; it would undermine 'the impression he makes' (p. 102). But it is different for an 'intellectual' hero (p. 103). He must have 'the last word'; this is what makes him 'immortal' (p. 103). Whereas the 'ordinary tragic hero' can just confront death courageously, a Socrates cannot be 'silent in the crisis of death', as it would 'have weakened the effect of his life' (p. 103). And Abraham, as 'the father of faith', needed to say something 'at the final moment' (p. 104). Of course, it seems a '**self-contradiction**' to hold that he should, as it appears to place him 'outside the paradox'; but, to the extent that I can comprehend the paradox, I can 'understand Abraham's total presence in that word', which has 'the **form of irony**', of saying something, but not saying anything (pp. 104–5). Abraham's reply shows 'the double movement' in his soul (p. 105). He makes 'the infinite movement of resignation': he knows that 'Isaac is to be sacrificed', and that he will do it (p. 105). But then he makes 'the movement of faith by virtue of the absurd': 'God could do something entirely different' (p. 105). 'I can perhaps understand Abraham', but only as one 'understands the paradox' (p. 105). I know I lack the 'courage' to act and speak as he did, which is 'the only miracle' (p. 105).

His own age and subsequent ones have greatly 'admired him', but no one understood him (p. 105). What was his achievement? He was 'true to his love', and the one who 'loves God' needs nothing else: he 'forgets the suffering in the love' (p. 106). Indeed, he forgets the suffering, but 'God himself' remembers it (p. 106). So, either there is 'a paradox', that the single individual 'stands in an absolute relation to the absolute, or Abraham is lost' (p. 106).

Epilogue (pp. 107–9)

Are we so certain we have reached 'the highest' that all we
have to do is fool ourselves into thinking we have not, so
that there is still something left to do (p. 107)? No generation 'learns the genuinely human' from previous ones; so, no
generation learns 'how to love from another' (p. 107). The
'highest' human passion is faith, and here 'every generation
begins from the beginning', and gets 'no further' than previous ones: 'the task is always sufficient for a lifetime' (p. 108).
In each generation, many do not come close to it, and 'nobody
goes further' (p. 108). I may not 'come to faith' for 'a long
time', but life has 'tasks enough', and will 'not be wasted',
if one 'honestly loves them' (p. 108). One who reaches faith
'does not come to a standstill' in it (pp. 108–9). He would be
'shocked' if someone suggested this, for he would reply, 'I am
not standing still at all since I have my life in it' (p. 109).

Overview

The following section is a chapter-by-chapter overview of Kierkegaard's *Fear and Trembling*, designed for quick reference to the Detailed Summary above. Readers may also find this section helpful for revision.

A Dialectical Lyric by Johannes de silentio

Preface (pp. 3–6)

Johannes de silentio explains that, currently, there is a clearance sale of ideas, with everybody associated with philosophy easily going beyond mere doubting. It is claimed this is what Descartes did, but his doubt did not extend to faith, nor did he tell everyone to doubt. Previously, faith was seen as a lifelong task and, at the end of their lives, old people could still recall the fear and trembling that had brought discipline to their youth. But now, to go further, everyone begins at the point they reached. The present writer is not a philosopher, but believes that putting the whole content of faith into conceptual form would not mean it had been understood. He considers writing a luxury, made more enjoyable by few people reading his output. He knows that, in an age when books are expected not to challenge conventional opinion, he will be ignored or criticized.

Tuning Up (pp. 7–11)

A man who had heard the story of Abraham as a child, found his enthusiasm for it increased as he got older, but he understood it less. He wanted to go up Mount Moriah with Abraham and

Isaac. He was no intellectual, and did not feel compelled to go beyond faith, thinking it enviable to possess it.

I (pp. 8–9) Rising early, Abraham took Isaac with him and, after riding silently for three days, saw Mount Moriah in the distance. Taking only Isaac, he decided he would not hide from him where everything was leading. As he blessed him, he looked paternal, and spoke encouragingly, but Isaac did not understand, and begged for his life. Abraham turned away and, when Isaac saw his face next, his appearance was frightful. Throwing Isaac to the ground, he denied he was his father, and called himself an idolater, who was about to carry out, not God's command, but his own desire. Trembling, Isaac begged God for mercy, and to be his father. Abraham thanked God; it was better Isaac should believe him a monster than lose faith in God. When weaning a child, the mother blackens her breast, so it does not look attractive. The child will think the breast has changed, but not the mother, who is still loving. It is good fortune not to need worse measures to wean a child.

II (p. 9) Rising early, Abraham embraced Sarah, and she kissed Isaac. The two rode in silence, and Abraham's eyes were fixed on the ground, until he looked up to see Mount Moriah. He bound Isaac, and drew the knife, but then saw the ram God had chosen. After sacrificing it, he returned home, but could not forget what God had demanded of him. Isaac flourished, but Abraham did not experience joy again. When weaning a child, the mother covers her breast, so the child no longer has a mother. A child is fortunate, if he does not lose his mother in some other way.

III (p. 10) Rising early, Abraham kissed Sarah, and she kissed Isaac. Riding along thoughtfully, Abraham thought of Hagar and the son he had turned out into the desert. After climbing Mount Moriah, he drew the knife. He rode to Mount Moriah again, more than once, to beg God's forgiveness for forgetting a father's duty, and being willing to sacrifice Isaac, but found no peace of mind. If it was a sin, he did not see how it could be forgiven, as there was no worse one. When a child is weaned, the mother is also sorrowful, as her child will no longer be so close, and they jointly mourn this brief sorrow. Fortunate is the mother who kept the child so close and did not need to sorrow more.

IV (pp. 10–1) In the early morning, Abraham bade farewell to Sarah. When they reached Mount Moriah, Abraham prepared everything calmly but, as he drew the knife, Isaac saw his hand was clenched in despair, though he still drew it. They returned home, but Isaac had lost faith. He spoke to nobody about what he had seen, and Abraham did not suspect he had seen it. When a child is to be weaned, the mother provides solid food. She is fortunate, who has this stronger nourishment handy. The man thought about the story of Abraham and, on returning home from a pilgrimage to Mount Moriah, declared that no one was as great as Abraham, although no one could understand him.

A Tribute to Abraham (pp. 12–20)

Without a sense of the eternal, human life would just be one of despair. But, just as he created man and woman, God made the hero and the poet and orator. The latter is happy, as he can admire the former, who is his better nature, and celebrate him in song and speech. This unites him with the hero, who loves him equally, as he is the hero's better nature: feeble, yet glorified. So, no one great will ever be forgotten. Everyone is great in his own way, in proportion to the greatness of what he loved, whether himself or others; but the one who loved God became greater than everybody. Each will be remembered, but for greatness proportionate to the scale of what he struggled with. Struggling with the world brings the greatness of conquering it; struggling with oneself, the greatness of self-conquest; struggling with God means being greater than everybody. Conquest in the world is by power, but conquest of God is by powerlessness. Greatness can come through power, wisdom, hope or love, but Abraham was greater than everyone, through that power whose strength is powerlessness; that wisdom whose secret is folly; that hope whose form is madness; that love that is hatred of oneself.

When Abraham became a foreigner in the promised land, he left worldly wisdom behind, and took faith with him; otherwise, he would not have gone. He was God's chosen one but, given the pain involved, someone banished from God's grace would have understood his situation better. He may have bemoaned his situation, as is human; but it is greater to believe. In faith, he received the promise that he would be the forefather of the world's generations, and he went on believing it, even when his own and Sarah's age made it ridiculous to think they would have a child. He might have faltered, and told God, without bitterness, that he could see God's promise was not going to be fulfilled. He would have been remembered for his example, but would not have become the father of faith. However, things happened as he believed they would.

Abraham had kept his faith, but God tested him again, by ordering him to sacrifice Isaac. God had made the preposterous come true, but was now bringing it to nothing. But Abraham's faith was not the kind that gives up easily. It related to this life: that he would grow old in the promised land, and then be remembered forever through Isaac. He believed, and believed in the absurd. He would still have been admired and remembered, if he had doubted, gone to Mount Moriah, and, asking God not to despise his sacrifice, though it was not of the best, plunged the knife into himself: but he would not be an inspiration to the anguished. He believed, and did not appeal to God to withdraw his command. Indeed, the Bible says that, when God called him, he replied cheerfully, confidently and trustingly. He was not one who, in adversity, drags himself along. Telling nobody, he hurried off to Mount Moriah, as if to a celebration. Many fathers, who have lost a child, have lost all hope for the future; but, at least, the loss was not their fault. Abraham's situation was worse, as he was responsible for Isaac's fate. But he knew that no sacrifice was too hard when God demanded it. If he had doubted, and then seen the ram before drawing the knife, and sacrificed it, he could have kept Isaac. But things would have been very different. He would have been a witness, not to his own faith or God's grace, but only to the frightfulness of ascending Mount Moriah, which would have been remembered as the place where Abraham doubted. So, Abraham returned home, having gained everything, and kept Isaac; and he is honoured still. He was the first to bear witness to the struggle with God; and, in a life that lasted 150 years, got no further than faith.

Problems (pp. 21–107)

A preliminary outpouring from the heart (pp. 21–46)

There is a saying that only one who works gets bread, but it is not always so in the ordinary world, where people do not necessarily get what they deserve. However, in the spiritual world, which is under God's eternal rule, the sun does not shine equally on the good and the evil, and only the one who is prepared to draw the knife gets Isaac. Some people want the spiritual world to be like the ordinary one, so that no effort is needed. Those who do not want to make an effort, but wish to understand the story of Abraham, present it in ordinary terms. Abraham loved God so much he was willing to sacrifice the best to him; but 'the best' is a vague term. If the rich young man Jesus met had sold what he had to help the poor, he would be praised for giving up the best, but would not have suffered Abraham's anxiety, as there is no ethical obligation to money, like that of a father's duty to his son. And if someone tried to follow Abraham's example, a member of the clergy would condemn him as social outcast for wanting to murder his son, even though he had preached about, and praised, the example of Abraham in church. Such a man might be deterred by the clergyman's rebuke, but one who refused to heed it would end up being executed, or sent to an insane asylum.

It seems as if only Abraham is entitled to be a great man, who performed a great deed, while those who try to copy him commit a great sin. This needs to be thought about carefully before praise is heaped on Abraham. If faith does not make willingness to murder one's son a holy act, Abraham must be judged in the same way as anybody else. In ethical terms, he intended to murder Isaac, in religious terms, to sacrifice him. If faith is taken out, Abraham's intention to murder his son remains, and someone without faith could imitate that. However, even if it is accepted that Abraham was a murderer, it would not necessarily stop him being revered. But does talking about Abraham create the risk that stupid people might copy him? Even though the present age is not abundant in faith, it is safe to talk of him, provided all the emphasis is on his faith. It is through faith, not murder, that one can come to be like Abraham.

If I were going to preach about Abraham, I would start with his being a devout and god-fearing man, who was worthy to be God's chosen one, and whose love for his son few fathers could match. And, if someone, having heard about the frightfulness of Abraham's deed, wanted to copy him, I would accompany him, and explain that he could withdraw from so severe a trial, and leave it to God to take Isaac, if he wanted him. I believe that such a person could come to be favourably regarded, but he would be severely judged, even in times of great faith. Having made my audience aware of the intense inner debate and tremendous passion that faith involves, I would not let them think they had found a man of high faith, to whom they could attach themselves, but would stress how hard it is to make the movement of faith.

Poets talk of love, not faith, and even theology just seeks philosophy's approval, and acknowledges the difficulties of understanding Hegel. But Hegel is easy to grasp, compared to Abraham; his life is such an extraordinary paradox. I can identify myself with, and think myself into, the mind of a hero, but not into Abraham's. It is not that I think faith insignificant. I know about the frightful but, even if I approach it bravely, it is not with the courage of faith. I find it impossible to plunge confidently into the absurd. I know that God is love, but lack the courage of belief. God's love seems to be on a different scale to the ordinary world. I lack the joy of faith, which is convinced of God's concern for the least thing.

Can anyone now make the movement of faith? Had I, as a tragic hero, been called to Mount Moriah, I would not have shirked it. But I would have bemoaned my situation, and the imminent loss of all my joy, and resignation would not have been a substitute for faith. I would not have loved Isaac as Abraham did, and would have held back. This would have put me in an awkward position when I received Isaac again, as I could not have been joyful with him. Abraham, however, though willing to sacrifice Isaac, always believed that God would not demand him; and he believed this by virtue of the absurd, because he had no reason to think that God, having demanded Isaac, would revoke his command. No doubt, the outcome surprised him but, by a double movement, he recovered his original position, and so could receive Isaac joyfully.

Even if he had sacrificed Isaac, he would still have believed, not in future happiness, but in this-worldly happiness, with God giving him another Isaac, or restoring him to life. To lose everything, and then regain it, through the absurd, is shocking, but is the only miracle. Faith's inner debate, of which I have some idea, is the finest, but I can only move so far towards it. Abraham received Isaac back with delight, without needing time to come to terms with what had happened. He loved God with faith, and so considered God, not himself. He went beyond infinite resignation, and reached faith. This age will not stop at faith, but it would be best, if it did. The movement of faith must be made by virtue of the absurd, but so that the finite is not lost, but gained in its entirety. I can make the movements towards the infinite but, miraculously, faith, after making these, makes the movements back towards the world; and, unlike the knights of infinite resignation, those who have faith look like ordinary, relatively uncultured, middle-class people.

If I knew where to find a knight of faith, I would go to see him, so I could learn from him. He would probably be surprisingly like a tax collector, showing no trace of the infinite. He would seem to belong entirely to the world, and to be leading a thoroughly conventional life, just letting things take their course. But he does nothing, except by virtue of the absurd and, every moment, is making the movement of infinity. He has experienced the pain of renouncing what was dearest to him in the world, but he can delight in the finite as much as one who never knew anything higher. He has resigned everything infinitely, and then seized it back again by virtue of the absurd. Though always making the movement of infinity, he does it so deftly that he gets finitude out of it. Unlike those who focus on the infinite, and who seem strangers to the ordinary world, he can express the sublime in the pedestrian.

As an example, there is the story of a young man who falls in love with a princess, but has no hope of gaining her. The knight of infinite resignation, having first satisfied himself of the genuineness of his love, does not forget about it, but reconciles himself with the turn life has taken. His love for the princess is transformed into love of God, which nothing that happens in this world can take away. People say that everything is possible for human beings. This may be true, spiritually speaking, but not in the ordinary world. By expressing his love spiritually, the knight of infinite resignation is renouncing it and, once he has done so, the princess is lost. Infinite resignation gives peace and rest, and those who have not diminished themselves, can make this movement which, in its pain, will reconcile them with existence. Each individual must make the movement for himself, and it is neither easy, nor instantly achievable. We would laugh at novice dancers, who thought they could perform a dance immediately, just because previous generations had learned the steps; but such is people's attitude to the spiritual world. Infinite resignation is the last stage before faith, and those who have not made this movement will not have it. Only in infinite resignation does the individual understand what he really is, and become capable of taking hold of existence by virtue of faith.

In this story, the knight of faith, like the knight of infinite resignation, gives up his love, and is reconciled to this in pain. But then he makes a more wonderful movement, saying he believes he will win the princess by virtue of the absurd as, for God, everything is possible. Now, the absurd is not the same as the improbable or unforeseen. In the ordinary world, the knight of faith's goal was impossible. He could be saved only by the absurd, taken hold of by faith. While accepting the impossibility, he believes the absurd. Faith is not a spontaneous emotion, but the paradox of existence. The movement of infinite resignation requires strength, energy and spiritual freedom, but the next movement, getting everything by virtue of the absurd, is a miracle. But, just as I want to make this movement, I am seized by a monstrous anxiety, for is it tempting God? And this is the movement of faith that theology wants to sell off cheaply.

Resignation, from which comes awareness of the eternal, does not require faith; but to go further does, and this is the paradox. The movements of resignation and faith are easily confused. Someone complains of loss of faith, but has only reached the point when he should make the movement of resignation. I give up nothing by faith, but receive everything. Renouncing the whole world of time and space, to gain the eternal, demands purely human courage, but grasping it, by virtue of the absurd, requires the paradoxical and humble courage of faith. Abraham did not renounce Isaac by faith, but received him by it. The rich young man should have given up his possessions through resignation. Then the knight of faith might have told him that, if he could believe it, he would get them all back by virtue of the absurd. One can resign everything by one's own strength and find peace and rest in pain. One can save one's soul, if seeking love of God, rather than worldly happiness. But one's own strength will not enable one to obtain the smallest bit of what belongs to finitude. It enables one to give up the princess, and find joy in the pain, but not to get her back, because resignation has exhausted one's strength. It is by faith, by virtue of the absurd, that one will get her. One, incapable of making this movement, returns to the pain of resignation. Having the princess would be glorious, and the knight of faith is happy, and heir to the finite, while the knight of resignation is a stranger there. If all those of the present generation who seek to go beyond faith are reconciled in and by pain, have performed the miraculous, and grasped the whole of existence by virtue of the absurd, then they should be saluted. But it is hard to see why they refuse to stop at faith and, if they have it, to understand why they are ashamed to admit it.

People must not give others the impression that faith is lowly or easy. Some people look at the Abraham story differently, interpreting it as a trial, and praising God for returning Isaac to him. As a result, it becomes a trivial episode. Once he sees the ram, it will all be over. But, either Abraham should be forgotten about, or the prodigious paradox that is the meaning of his life should be fully appreciated, so that the present age can understand that it can be joyful if it has faith. The greatness of Abraham's achievement, in holding on to his belief, must be recognized, so that people can decide if they are equal to being similarly tested. There is no reason to fear the story will make people want to be tried like Abraham, but it is wrong to peddle a cheap edition of the story, and tell them not to do the same. The dialectical factors in the Abraham story must be explored, so that the prodigious paradox that is faith, which can turn murder into a holy act well pleasing to God, and restore Isaac to Abraham, can be grasped. Thought cannot do so, for faith begins where thinking stops.

Problem I: Is there a teleological suspension of the ethical? (pp. 46–59)

It is accepted that ethical precepts are universal, and apply to everybody. The ethical has no end beyond itself, but is the end of everything outside itself, so it would be contradictory to say that the ethical could be set aside, to serve a higher purpose. The individual finds his end in the universal, and his task is to express himself in it, abolishing his own individuality, in order to become the universal. Affirming his individuality against the universal is a sin and, after submitting to the universal, the individual, who wishes to do so, is in a state of temptation, from which he can only free himself by complete surrender to the universal. If we agree with this, Hegel is right to regard individuality as a moral form of evil, which must be eliminated, and to hold that the individual, who remains so, either sins or stands in temptation. But this makes Hegel wrong not to denounce Abraham as a murderer. Faith's paradox is that the individual, as such, is higher than the universal and, as an individual, stands in an absolute relation to God. Though inaccessible to thought, faith is this paradox, or it has never existed, and Abraham and faith are lost. The individual may confuse it with temptation, but faith should not be turned into something else, for the sake of those who do not have it. They should admit to not having it, while those who do should state criteria for distinguishing this paradox from a temptation.

There is this teleological suspension of the ethical in the

story of Abraham, the representative of faith. He acts by virtue of the absurd, which is that he, the single individual, is higher than the universal. There is no escaping the paradox: if Abraham tried to do so, he would have to admit to being in a state of temptation. Either he does not sacrifice Isaac or, if he does, must repentantly return to the universal. He gets Isaac back again, by virtue of the absurd, and is no tragic hero, but either a murderer or a believer. But it could be the case that the story contains a higher ethical purpose that justifies suspending the ethical. There is no lack of examples. When, in a national crisis, a god demands a young girl as sacrifice, people understand, as with Agamemnon and Iphigenia, that the father must make it. When Jephthah's vow to God meant sacrificing his own daughter, everybody understood that he must honour it. People will admire a father like Brutus, who punished his son for failing in his duty. But they would not understand if Agamemnon had sacrificed Iphigenia when there was no need; if Jephthah had decided to sacrifice his daughter on a whim; or if Brutus had put a righteous son to death. And they would have been amazed if these heroes had asserted that nothing would happen, and that they believed this, by virtue of the absurd. The difference between the tragic hero and Abraham is that the former remains within the ethical. In these examples, the ethical is suspended for a higher ethical purpose, and there is no question of the ethical being teleologically suspended.

But Abraham suspended the ethical for a higher purpose outside the ethical. His act cannot be brought into relation to the universal, apart from his having overstepped it. His was an individual decision. The tragic hero's greatness lies in ethical virtue, but Abraham's is in personal virtue. There is no higher expression of the ethical, in Abraham's life, than the father's duty to love his son. But Abraham acts for God's sake and his own: because God demands proof and faith, and so he can prove his faith. Usually, the temptation is not to perform an ethical duty, but, with Abraham, the ethical itself is the temptation, as it would have stopped him doing God's will.

Thus, Abraham belongs in a new category. The tragic hero does not have this private relation with the divine. For him, the ethical is the divine, and the ethical is suspended for a higher ethical purpose. But, with Abraham, there is no higher ethical purpose to justify his disregarding the ethical. He has set aside a universal ethical precept, to grasp something higher. If he is mistaken, or has misunderstood God, there can be no salvation for him. The tragic hero performs his exploit at a certain point in time, but is forever able to make others forget their sufferings in his. Abraham is different. One approaches him with awe and anxiety, all too aware that he may be wrong. It is hard to comprehend the condition of one who thus suspends the ethical for a higher purpose outside the ethical. As the individual, who has set aside the universal, Abraham seems to have sinned and, if his action cannot be construed in a way that is not sin, judgement has to be against him. The paradox, which he cannot explain to anyone else, is that, as the single individual, he put himself in an absolute relation to God. If he can be justified, it is by being the individual, not the universal.

It is hard to see how the individual can be certain he is justified. Subordinating individuality to the state or society rules out the paradox of the individual being higher than the universal. If a hero offends society, by becoming a paradox it does not understand, he may argue that the outcome will justify him. This is the line taken by the minor academics, who presume to judge great men. But they do not realize that one needs to pay attention to the beginning. The hero only knows how splendid the outcome is, when his deed is done. Yet, people are eager to know it, rather than the anxiety, the distress and the paradox. But it is what the individual does, not what happens to him, that makes him great. No one is great because he won a lottery. What makes a person great is the anxiety and distress which tests him. Nobody was greater than Mary, Jesus' mother, but she was not made great just by being one who was favoured among women: the distress, the anxiety, and the paradox are left out. The angel did not tell other women in Israel not to despise her because something extraordinary was happening to her. So, nobody understood her. She is great because she was content to be God's handmaid and, just as Abraham did not require sympathy, she did not ask for admiration. Both became greater through their distress and torment. It sounds as if it would have been wonderful to have seen Jesus on earth, but it is easy to forget the anxiety, the distress and the paradox. Eighteen centuries later, it is easy enough to become a disciple, but not then. Before the outcome, either Abraham was a murderer, or we are confronted by an extraordinary paradox. For his story contains a teleological suspension of the ethical: a single individual, he rose higher than the universal. One can become a tragic hero through one's own strength, but not a knight of faith. Faith is a miracle, from which none is excluded. It is a passion, and passion unites all human life.

Problem II: Is there an absolute duty to God (pp. 59–71)

It is said that the ethical is the universal, and so is the divine, so every duty is a duty to God. But this means there is no duty to God, as duty does not involve a relation to God. Talk of a duty to love God is a mere tautology, because 'God' just means 'duty', and so he comes to have only ethical power. This approach makes wanting to love God, in some other way, look suspicious. If there is nothing exceptional in human life, except what is there accidentally, Hegel is right; but then Abraham cannot be faith's father. For Hegel, the outer is higher than the inner, but the paradox of faith is that it is the other way around. The ethical view of life requires the individual to remove his inner qualities, and express them in outward form. But, faith involves a new inwardness, which does not fit in with the external. Recent philosophy lumps faith in with feeling and mood, but it is preceded by a movement of infinity, which begins unexpectedly, by virtue of the absurd. It is only when the individual has exhausted himself in the infinite that faith can break forth.

Faith's paradox is the individual being higher than the universal, determining his relation to it by his relation to God, not the other way round. This also means there is an absolute duty to God, in which the individual relates himself to God absolutely. And, if duty to God is absolute, the ethical becomes relative, and its expression paradoxical, such that loving God can lead the knight of faith to love his neighbour in ways that are at odds with his ethical duty. Here is the paradox of the Abraham story. Ethically, the father must love the son, but this ethical relation becomes relative, beside the absolute relation to God. When someone performs an act that does not conform to the universal, people think he does it for his own, not God's sake. So, it is both supremely egotistical and the most absolute devotion to God. But, if faith has to express itself through the universal, it is annulled. Because of this paradox, the single individual cannot make himself understood. Nor can one knight of faith help another; either the individual

Overview

becomes one, by assuming the paradox, or he never does. The greatness and the frightfulness of becoming a knight of faith is that one can only do so as a single individual.

There is a hard saying in Luke's Gospel about absolute duty to God and Jesus involving hating one's whole family. This is sometimes watered down, but must be understood literally: God demands absolute love. Talk of hate here is a paradox. Absolute duty to God may lead one to do what ethics would forbid, but cannot make the knight of faith stop loving. Hatred is the ethical term for Abraham, as he prepared to sacrifice Isaac but, as God demands him, Abraham must love him, even more dearly; only then can he sacrifice him. It is his love for Isaac, in paradoxical opposition to his love for God, which makes his act a sacrifice. His distress and anxiety in the paradox preclude his making himself understood, but he only sacrifices Isaac when his act is in absolute contradiction to his feelings. However, the reality of his act belongs to the universal, and there he is a murderer.

Fear of the consequences of individuals behaving as individuals explains the reluctance to draw attention to passages like the one from Luke. The prevailing view is that people should be forced into becoming the universal. But fearing to mention such passages is to fear mentioning Abraham. Further, one who is concerned for his soul believes that to live in the world, under one's own supervision, is to live strictly. One must show one is not a wild animal, who needs coercion, by speaking with fear and trembling. While the tragic hero resigns himself, to express the universal, the knight of faith resigns the universal, to become the single individual. Far from finding this easy, he is only too conscious of the glory of belonging to the universal; of being intelligible to himself in the universal; and of having others understand it through

73

him. He knows, too, the loneliness and frightfulness of being outside the universal. Abraham may well have wished that his task were just to love Isaac, as a father should, and that any sacrifice of him was for the universal, to inspire others. But he knows he is being tested himself, and can do nothing for the universal. And he cannot explain it further: his life is subject to God's command, and not in the public domain. While the tragic hero can be secure in the universal, the knight of faith is constantly tried and tempted by awareness that he can return repentantly to the universal. The tragic hero, although he transcends the ethical, still has a place of refuge in the universal; but the knight of faith is alone in everything. Abraham has no place of refuge in the universal. He must concentrate his soul back on the miracle of faith. Without that, he is just like Agamemnon: as long as he can justify willingness to sacrifice Isaac, when he does not thereby benefit the universal.

Only the individual can decide whether he is a knight of faith, or just in a state of temptation, but the former has a distinguishing characteristic. While the true knight of faith is in absolute isolation, the false one cannot bear the frightfulness of being a single individual, and tries to join with others. The true knight, while feeling the pain of being unable to make himself intelligible to others, has no wish to instruct them. The false knight does not realize that a true knight is a witness, not a teacher, and is eager to share what he thinks he knows with others. Either there is an absolute duty to God, and this is the paradox: that the single individual stands in an absolute relation to God; or faith has never existed and Abraham is lost.

Overview

Problem III: Was it ethically defensible of Abraham to conceal his undertaking from Sarah, from Eliezer, from Isaac? (pp. 71–106)

The ethical is the universal and the disclosed, whereas the single individual is the concealed, whose responsibility is to become disclosed in the universal. Unless the single individual, as the particular, can be higher than the universal, Abraham's behaviour cannot be defended. Hegel's philosophy admits of no justified concealment, and requires disclosure, but is then inconsistent in considering Abraham to be the father of faith. The question can be examined purely aesthetically, in the category of the interesting, which is on the boundary between aesthetics and ethics. In drama, wherever recognition is mentioned, prior concealment is implied. But, as modern drama has dispensed with fate, concealment and disclosure are the hero's free act, for which he is responsible. I want to make it clear that aesthetic concealment and the paradox are completely different. Imagine two young people, who have not told each other of their love. They are responsible aesthetically for choosing to conceal their love. However, aesthetics trades in sentiment, so a coincidence reveals their true feelings, and they get each other. Ethics, on the other hand, disdains sentimentality and coincidence, and deplores the existence of a secret the lovers have assumed on their own responsibility. Thus, aesthetics demanded concealment and rewarded it; ethics demanded disclosure and punished concealment. By his silence, the tragic hero takes on a responsibility as the single individual, while ethics requires that he constantly express the universal. Yet, the inner qualities of secrecy and silence can make for greatness in a person. The paradox is that they could be divine or demonic. Silence can be both the devil's trap and God's way of communicating with the single individual.

Detailed summary of Fear and Trembling

Before going back to Abraham, I shall discuss a few poetic characters, whose anxiety may shed some light. Aristotle has a story of a man, who is told that his marriage will bring him misfortune, and decides not to marry. The actual incident ended badly, but it is possible to think of a number of things a man could do in such a situation. He could say nothing, marry, and hope for the best; say nothing and not marry; or speak out. Ethics would require him to speak. As he obtained the information from the Oracle at Delphi, he would have been understood so, if he chooses silence, it is because, as the single individual he wants to be higher than the universal. However, if he had obtained this knowledge privately, he could not speak, however much he wished to, not because, as a single individual, he wanted to place himself in an absolute relation to the universal, but because he had been placed as the single individual in an absolute relation to the absolute. The legend of Agnes and the Merman provides an example along the lines of the demonic. The merman confronts the dilemma of whether to opt for concealment or disclosure. While he seems to have evidence that his silence is justified, as he suffers all his pain in it, he can speak, and become a grand tragic hero by doing so. If he is rescued out of the demonic in repentance for his sin, two paths are open to him. By remaining concealed, he will not come as the single individual into an absolute relation to the demonic, but will fall back on the counter-paradox that God will save Agnes; or he could be saved by Agnes, in that he is saved insofar as he becomes disclosed. When the individual has, by guilt and sin, come outside the universal, he can only return to it, by having come as the single individual into an absolute relation to God. In sin, the individual is already higher, in the direction of the demonic paradox, than the universal. An ethics that ignores

sin is a futile discipline but, if it affirms its existence, it goes
beyond itself. As to the merman, if he lets himself be saved
by Agnes, he is the greatest person imaginable, but he cannot
belong to Agnes unless, after the infinite movement of repentance, he makes the movement by virtue of the absurd. One
insufficient in passion to make either movement can easily
believe he has achieved the highest, and can help others do so,
because he can persuade himself that the world of spirit is like
a card game where everything happens by chance. Yet, if this
really is an age in which the highest is commonly achieved,
it is hard to see why there is general doubt about the immortality of the soul. One who has made merely the movement
of infinity scarcely doubts. Entering a monastery may not be
life's highest course, but there is no evidence of people pur-
suing a higher one today. Rather, a form of worldly wisdom
prevails, which deceives us into believing we have attained
the highest, and stops us even attempting lesser things. Only
one movement remains after the monastic: that of the absurd.
But few people today understand what the absurd is. Our age
needs the courage to believe in the power of the spirit, and to
stop cravenly stifling its better impulses and enviously stifling
them in others. It needs an enthusiastic figure to remind it of
what it has forgotten.

In the Book of Tobit, Tobias wants to marry Sarah, but she
knows that an evil demon will kill the bridegroom on the
wedding night. This made her very unfortunate: it is hard
not to find someone to whom one can give oneself, but even
harder not to be able to give oneself. If a poet used this story,
he would focus on Tobias' heroic courage in thus risking his
life, but Sarah is the heroine. She shows ethical maturity and
humility, in allowing the one she loves to take such a risk on
her behalf, and great faith in God, that she will not hate one to

whom she owes so much. A man would find it difficult to be in that position. A proud nature can endure anything, including punishment for sin, but not pity; and Sarah is bound to be pitied. What made Shakespeare's Gloucester a demoniac was being unable to bear so much pity. Such people are placed outside the universal and society by nature or circumstance. They are not to blame for it, but it is the beginning of the demonic in them.

The legend of *Faust* also features an individual, who wants to save the universal by concealment and silence. The doubter par excellence, he knows he would terrify others, if he shared his doubt, and he does not tell Margaret of his love for her either. In silence, he sacrifices himself, as he knows that speaking will put everything into disorder. Ethics condemns his silence, demanding acknowledgement of the universal, and accusing him of acting from hidden pride. But if he can become the single individual, who as the particular stands in an absolute relation to the absolute, he can obtain authorization for his silence. The New Testament accepts such a silence. In the Sermon on the Mount, we are told that, when fasting, we should anoint our heads and wash our faces, so that others will not notice.

This highlights Abraham's unintelligibility, and there is no analogy that helps to explain him. He did not speak to Sarah, Eliezer or Isaac, even though for him, there was no higher expression of the ethical than family life. Aesthetics would permit the single individual to keep silent to save another, but Abraham is not silent for Isaac's sake. He is sacrificing him for his own and God's sake, and thus offends against aesthetics, which can accommodate sacrifice of self, and silence about it, but not sacrifice of another for one's own sake. But ethics demands disclosure. The genuine tragic hero sacrifices himself for the universal. So, here is the paradox: either the single individual can have an absolute relation to God, meaning ethics is not the highest, or Abraham, neither a tragic, nor an aesthetic, hero, is lost.

Abraham cannot speak, wherein is his distress and anxiety. Speaking translates one into the universal. Abraham can talk of his love for Isaac, but not of his willingness to sacrifice him. Nobody can understand his trial, for Sarah, Eliezer and Isaac would ask him why he was going to do this deed, and could not just leave it. This is where he differs from the tragic hero, who is unfamiliar with the frightful responsibility of solitude. He cannot speak, because he speaks in a divine language. Of course, he could stop at any moment, and repent the whole thing as a temptation. Then, he could speak, and be understood; but he would no longer be Abraham. So, he cannot explain that his trial is one where the ethical is the temptation, as he has left the sphere of the universal. He makes two movements: the infinite one of resignation, in giving up Isaac, which cannot be understood, because it is a private undertaking, and that of faith. The latter is his consolation, as he tells himself that God will provide a new Isaac by virtue of the absurd. Only Abraham's reply to Isaac has been preserved: that God would provide the lamb. There is the question of whether it is appropriate for a tragic hero to make a final remark. Not if the significance of his life is in an external deed; it would undermine the impression he makes. But, an intellectual hero is different. He must have the last word; it is what makes him immortal. Whereas the ordinary tragic hero can just face death courageously, a Socrates cannot be silent, as it would have weakened the effect of his life. Abraham, as the father of faith, needed to say something at the final moment. Of course, it seems self-contradictory to say he should, as it appears to place him outside the paradox. But, to the extent that I can comprehend the paradox, I can understand Abraham's total presence in his reply, which says something, but yet does not say anything. His words show the double movement in his soul. He makes the infinite movement of resignation: he knows that Isaac is to be sacrificed, and that he will do it. But then he makes the movement of faith by virtue of the absurd: God could do something entirely different. Perhaps, I can understand Abraham, but only as one understands the paradox. I know I lack the courage to act and speak as he did, which is the only miracle. His own and subsequent ages have greatly admired him, but no one understood him. His achievement was to be true to his love, and the one who loves God needs nothing else: he forgets the suffering in the love. Indeed, he forgets the suffering, but God remembers. So, either there is a paradox: that the single individual stands in an absolute relation to God; or Abraham is lost.

Epilogue (pp. 107–109)

No generation learns the genuinely human from previous ones, so no generation learns how to love from another. The highest human passion is faith, and here every generation begins from the beginning, and gets no further than previous ones: the task is always sufficient for a lifetime. In each generation, many do not come close to it, and nobody goes further. One may not come to faith for a long time, but life has tasks enough, and will not be wasted, if one honestly loves them. One who reaches faith does not come to a standstill in it. He would be shocked if someone suggested this, for he would reply that he was not standing still at all since he had his life in it.

Glossary

A witness, never a teacher. One who bears witness to the (religious) truth, but does not try to instruct/impose it upon others.

Abraham (possibly third millennium BC). The story of Abraham, which consists of a number of legendary narratives, is found in Genesis 11.27–25.18. In response to God's call, Abraham left his home in Ur of Chaldees, and migrated to the land of Canaan (the promised land), where he settled. His life is characterized by his faith in, and obedience to, God, of which his willingness to sacrifice Isaac is an example. He is seen as the father of the Hebrew race and also of Judaism, Christianity and Islam.

Absolute. God, absolute spirit. See Context.

Actuality. Reality.

Agamemnon. In Homer's *Iliad*, the king of Mycenae and brother of Menelaus (king of Sparta and husband of Helen), who led the Greek army that attacked and defeated Troy.

Agent. One who performs an action.

Analogy. Drawing a parallel between two things on the basis of similarities between them.

Ancient Greeks. Thinkers, philosophers of ancient Greece.

Annul. Terminate, declare invalid.

Apex. Summit, climax.

Apostle. One sent forth to preach the Christian gospel, particularly the 12 disciples, chosen by Jesus.

Aristotle (384–322 BC). Athenian philosopher, student of Plato and author of such books as *De Interpretatione, Nicomachean Ethics* and *Metaphysics*. This story is from *Politics* V, 4.

Associate professors. Minor academics, who are unfit to judge great men.

Augur's pronouncement. Declaration/prediction by a professional foreteller of the future.

Authentic exemplar. One who is a genuine model or pattern (of a principle or attitude).

Blessing. Asking for God's help and protection for someone.

Book of Tobit (Tobias). Part of the Old Testament Apocrypha: writings that are not considered to have the same authority as the canonical books of the Old Testament.

Bourgeois philistinism. Uncultured attitude, associated with middle-class people, who are more interested in making money and material well-being than intellectual or artistic pursuits.

Brutus, Lucius Junius. In Roman tradition, he led the successful rebellion against his tyrannical uncle, Tarquinius Superbus, King of Rome, and had his own sons executed, when they tried to restore him.

Buber, Martin (1878–1965). Austrian-born Jewish philosopher, theologian and existentialist. After emigrating to Palestine in 1938, he became professor at the Hebrew University, Jerusalem, and played a major part in educational developments in the new State of Israel. His books include *I and Thou, On Judaism* and *Good and Evil*.

Caricatures of faith. Representing faith in an exaggerated or ridiculous way.

Glossary

Chosen one. The one whom God has chosen for a particular purpose. See Isaiah 42.1–4.

Christian world. The part of the world where Christianity is the only or dominant religion.

Clerical dignity. Stateliness appropriate to position as member of clergy/minister of religion.

Comic (the). Humorous, what will make people laugh.

Common expression for their suffering. The same experience of suffering awaiting them: misfortune is foretold only for the bridegroom.

Communion. Here, communication, way of communicating.

Contradiction. Denial, the complete opposite.

Contrary to expectation. Contrary to what Abraham would have expected, given his advanced age.

Counter-paradox. See paradox below.

Daily bread of life. The comforts of everyday existence.

Deity. God.

Delphi/Delphic Oracle. The temple of Apollo at Delphi in Greece, where the priestess (the Pythia) answered questions on religious, moral and other issues. Answers to questions about future events were often capable of more than one interpretation.

Demonic/demoniac/demon. To do with demons, evil spirits.

Descartes, René (1596–1650). French rationalist philosopher, and author of *Meditations on First Philosophy*, *Discourse on Method* and *The Principles of Philosophy*. Descartes' method, in the *Meditations*, is to doubt everything that can possibly be doubted, including all his former beliefs, based on sense experience, in order to find something absolutely certain that could be a secure base for all knowledge.

Despair. Hopelessness.

Dialectic/dialectical. The process of critical discussion and argument about a subject/opinion that enables those taking part to gain knowledge/obtain truth about it; interaction of ideas that can make progress possible.

Disciple. Follower of Jesus. See apostles above.

Disdain. Scorn, decline to take notice of.

Disgrace. The fact that she (Sarah) had not had any children.

Divine. Of, relating to, God.

Doubt/doubting. Descartes' method of doubt, comprehensive doubt. See Descartes above.

Duty. That which the law, or a set of moral principles, requires/obliges us to do.

Earlier distorted knowledge. One of Descartes' reasons for doubting everything is that his senses sometimes deceive him: there is, for example, no infallible way of distinguishing what he sees in dreams from what he sees when awake.

Ecclesiastical hero. Champion of, one who has done great deeds for, the Church.

Egoism. Selfishness, preoccupation with the self.

Eliezer. Abraham's principal servant.

Emigrant. One who leaves one place to settle in another.

Ensnared/snare. Trapped/trap.

Esthetics (aesthetics). Study/appreciation of what is beautiful in nature, art or literature.

Esthetic (aesthetic) emotion. Feeling of the kind appropriate to contemplation of a work of art.

Eternal/eternity. Forever, that which always has existed and always will exist. In the Christian context, the idea that God transcends time: there is no past, present or future in God.

Eternal being. God.

Eternal consciousness. Awareness of the eternal.

Eternal divine order. God's eternal rule.

Eternal love. Everlasting love, divine love, love of God.

Eternal salvation. Human beings being saved by God, and given eternal life with him.

Ethical. That which relates to ethics. See the ethical is the universal below.

Ethical maturity. (Fully) developed understanding of what is right and wrong.

Ethical obligation. What one is required to do by a particular ethical precept.

Ethics. Set of moral principles/precepts that tell us what is right and wrong/what our duties are. See the ethical is the universal below.

Exegete. One who expounds, interprets (the Bible).

Existentialism. A philosophical approach that holds that, as the world lacks (or appears to) an ultimate purpose and does not offer human beings a clear set of beliefs, values or purposes, individuals must choose these for themselves.

External world. The real world, the world people actually inhabit.

Extravagant in faith. Abounding, immoderate in faith.

Faith. In a religious context, this can be simply religious belief/belief in God, or trusting belief in God (his existence and/or his goodness), and obedience of his commands.

Father of faith. One who exemplifies (complete) faith in God.

Favored among women. See Luke 1.28. The angel Gabriel addresses Mary as 'O favoured one, the Lord is with you!'

Fear and trembling. See Philippians 2.12: 'work out your own salvation with fear and trembling'.

Finitude. What is limited. See world of finitude below.

Flagrant. Open, blatant.

Folly. Foolishness. See 1 Corinthians 3.18–19: the wisdom of the world is foolishness to God, so things should not be judged by the world's standards.

Glossary

Form of irony. See irony below.

Form of knowledge. School of thought.

Form of sin. See sin below.

Freelancer. A self-employed writer, one who is free to write what he chooses.

Gloucester, Richard, Duke of. Central character of Shakespeare's play, *Richard III*, king of England 1483–5, who is believed to have murdered his nephews (the sons of Edward IV) to obtain the throne.

God. The Christian God, who is believed by Christians to be all-powerful (omnipotent), all-knowing (omniscient), infinitely benevolent/loving, and to have created the universe and all it contains from nothing.

God is love. See 1 John 4.8: 'He who does not love does not know God; for God is love.'

God's confidant. One in whom God trusts and confides.

God's will. What God commanded him to do.

Good and evil. See Matthew 5.45: God 'makes his sun rise on the evil and on the good'.

Grace. The help God freely gives to human beings.

Guiding star that rescues the anguished. A source of inspiration and guidance that saves those who are suffering severely (from religious doubts).

Hagar. Sarah's Egyptian maid, whom Sarah gave to Abraham as a mistress, and who bore him a son, Ishmael. See Genesis chapters 16 and 21.

Handmaid. How Mary describes herself. See Luke 1.38.

Hegel, Georg Wilhelm Friedrich (1770–1831). German philosopher, professor of philosophy at Berlin, and author of such works as *The Phenomenology of Mind* and *The Philosophy of Right*, whose ideas had a major impact on the course of philosophy in the nineteenth century.

Heterogeneous fraction. Element that is dissimilar, does not fit in.

Holy act. Act that is required by, devoted to, God.

Human consciousness. Human awareness, including of what is right or wrong.

Human pre-existence. Existing previously as a human being.

Hurry out of the world to which he did not belong. Abraham's faith in God did not make him want to leave this world (and its problems), in order to be with God in the next.

Hypocrite. One who pretends to be good/whose actions do not match his words.

Idea of fate. Events being predetermined.

Idolater. One who worships false gods.

Immediacy/immediate. That which is unmediated, direct, occurs at once or without delay.

Immortality of the soul. That the soul lives on after physical death. See soul below.

In his seed. In his descendants.

Incommensurable. Not comparable to in respect of size, not worthy to be measured with.

Incommensurability of genius. Exceptional intellectual abilities, which make an individual stand out from other people.

Infinite/infinity. Unlimited, without limit, relating to God, who is infinite.

Infinite resignation/resignation. Total acceptance of, acquiescence in, being reconciled with (all the problems and disappointments of) existence.

Iphigenia. Daughter of Agamemnon, king of Mycenae. When bad weather prevented the Greek fleet sailing for Troy, a soothsayer told Agamemnon he must sacrifice her to the goddess Artemis. However, Artemis took pity on her, and rescued her.

Irony. Giving what is said additional force, by using words with a literal meaning that is the opposite of what is meant.

Isaac. Son of Abraham and Sarah, husband of Rebekah and father of Esau and Jacob. The account of his intended sacrifice shows him as having complete trust in both God and Abraham. See Genesis 22.7–8.

Jephthah. See Judges chapters 11–12. Jephthah promised that, if he defeated the Ammonites, he would sacrifice the first person who came out to greet him on his return.

Jesus Christ (c. 5/6 BC–c. AD 30). Founder of Christianity, and believed by Christians to be the Son of God, who became incarnate (took on human nature).

Judge(s). Rulers of Israel before the establishment of the monarchy (Saul was the first king of Israel), who performed the functions of a king.

Kant, Immanuel (1724–1804). Influential German philosopher, whose writings cover metaphysics, moral philosophy and philosoply of religion, and include the *Critique of Pure Reason*, the *Critique of Practical Reason*, *Religion within the Boundaries of Mere Reason* and *The Groundwork of the Metaphysics of Morals*.

Kierkegaard, Michael Pedersen (1756–1838). Søren Kierkegaard's father, a shepherd boy from Jutland, who became a successful businessman in Copenhagen. His second wife, Anne, was the mother of Søren and his other children.

Knight of faith. Exponent/champion of faith.

Knight of infinite resignation. Exponent/champion of infinite resignation.

Law of indifference. The way the world operates: that people do not always get what they deserve.

Legend of Agnes and the Merman. A Danish legend.

Legend of Faust. The story of Faust, who sold his soul to the devil, in exchange for youth and worldly power.

Luke 14.26. The verse reads: 'If anyone comes to me and does not hate his own father and mother and wife and children and brothers and sisters, yes, and even his own life, he cannot be my disciple.'

Lyric. A type of poem that expresses individual thoughts or feelings.

Margaret. The young woman that Faust seduces.

Mediated. Not connected directly, but linked by something else.

Method. Descartes' method of doubt. See Descartes and earlier distorted knowledge above.

Mother of God. Mother of Jesus (see above).

Mount Moriah. In Genesis 22.2, Abraham is commanded to 'go to the land of Moriah', and offer Isaac as a sacrifice 'upon one of the mountains of which I shall tell you'.

Movement of faith. See faith above.

Movement of infinity. See infinite/infinity above.

Movement of resignation. See infinite resignation above.

Necessary condition. That which has to be present, in order for something else to exist.

New creation. See 2 Corinthians 5.17: 'if any one is in Christ, he is a new creation'.

Olsen. Regine (Schlegel) (1822–1904). Six years after Kierkegaard broke off his engagement to her, she married a civil servant, Johann Frederik Schlegel, who in 1855 (the year Kierkegaard died) became governor of the Danish West Indies.

Orator. (Gifted) public speaker.

Glossary

Paganism. Worship of false gods, absence of belief in Christianity.

Paltry. Worthless, contemptible.

Paradox. Statement/something that appears, but may not be, absurd or self-contradictory.

Paradox of existence. That things that seem impossible/cannot be attained in other ways can be achieved through faith/belief in the absurd (see below).

Paradox of faith. The apparently absurd and self-contradictory aspect of faith: that the single individual (see below) is higher than the universal.

Pariah of society. Social outcast.

Parson. Clergyman/minister of religion.

Particularity. Individuality, individual ethical principles.

Pensively. With serious thoughtfulness.

Philosopher. One who studies and practises/teaches philosophy.

Philosophy. Literally, love of wisdom. The study of ultimate reality, what really exists, the most general principles of things.

Placed outside the universal by nature or historical circumstance (people). Those whom their innate character or experiences in life have placed outside the claims of universal moral precepts. See the ethical is the universal below.

Play providence. Assume a responsibility that is beyond his competence/appropriate to God.

Powerlessness. See 2 Corinthians 12.9: '"my power is made perfect in weakness". I will all the more gladly boast of my weaknesses, that the power of Christ may rest upon me'.

Preposterous. Contrary to reason, absurd.

Promised land. The land God promised to Abraham and his descendants. See Genesis 17.8: 'I will give to you, and to your descendants ... all the land of Canaan, for an everlasting possession; and I will be their God'.

Public domain. Capable of being generally known/understood.

Put into conceptual form. Put into the form of ideas that can be expressed in language and fully understood.

Quadrille. A square dance for four couples.

Qualifications of inwardness. Qualities of/required for an inner life.

Qualitatively. In its quality.

Ram. Uncastrated male sheep, suitable for sacrifice.

Reducing all existence to the idea of the state or society. Subordinating individuality/individual identity to the (requirements of) the state or society, regarding/treating the individual as unimportant in comparison to the state or society.

Repentantly/repentance. Feeling sorrowful or regretful (usually for sin).

Responsible esthetically. Responsible in the context of the drama/play.

Rich young man. See Matthew 19.16–22. Jesus told the man, 'sell what you possess and give to the poor'.

Sacred duty. What must be done for religious reasons.

Sacrifice. Sacrifice was part of Judaism until the Romans destroyed the temple in Jerusalem in AD 70. However, human sacrifice was condemned from an early stage; but see Jephthah above.

Sarah. Abraham's wife, who went with him from Ur to the Land of Canaan, and who, according to God's promise, gave birth to Isaac when she was very old.

Sartre. Jean-Paul (1905–80). French existentialist philosopher, writer and playwright, whose works include the novel,

Nausea, Being and Nothingness and the influential lecture, *Existentialism and Humanism*.

Second father of the human race. See Genesis 12.2 ('And I will make of you a great nation') and Abraham above.

Sectarian. Here, wishing to create a sect or group of people who share the same religious view(s).

Self-contradiction. When what is asserted negates itself.

Sentimental discipline. An activity that involves emotions/feelings.

Sermon on the Mount. Jesus' ethical and religious teachings, which include the Beatitudes and the Lord's prayer, collected in Matthew, chapters 5–7, and presented in the form of a sermon delivered by Jesus.

Sin. Disobeying, offence against, the law of God.

Single individual. One person, the individual, in contrast to the universal.

Socrates. (c. 470–399 BC). Athenian philosopher, who devoted his life to pursuit of philosophical truth, but was executed for undermining belief in the gods and corrupting youth.

Solitude. Being entirely alone (and therefore having to decide things for oneself).

Soul. In Christianity, the spiritual element within human beings, which is the seat of personality and individual identity, which lives on after death, and which will be reunited with its body at the general resurrection.

Subjectivity. That which relates to the subject, the individual.

Tautological/tautology. Saying something twice in different ways.

Tax collector. A tax inspector: the knight of faith looks just like a civil servant.

Teleology. Concerned with end or purpose, the belief that things/events have an end or serve a purpose.

Teleologically suspended. Set aside, made not to apply (for a time), to serve a (higher) purpose.

Teleological suspension of the ethical. Setting aside universal moral laws, to serve a higher purpose: obeying God's commands.

Telos. End or purpose: morality has no end or purpose outside, or beyond, itself.

Temporality. The ordinary world and everything in it, which are subject to the law of time (and space).

Temptation. The temptation not to surrender to the universal. See the ethical is the universal below.

The absurd. Ridiculous, unreasonable: what faith (in God) demands or promises (often) seems ridiculous or unreasonable by worldly standards and may breach generally accepted moral precepts; that things that seem impossible/cannot be attained in other ways can be achieved through faith.

The ethical he has transcended teleologically. (The obedience to) a moral law or precept that he has gone beyond/set aside, in order to serve (what he considers to be) a higher purpose.

The ethical is the divine. What morality requires and God commands are identical.

The ethical is the temptation. For Abraham, the temptation is to follow universally accepted moral laws or precepts, rather than obey God's command.

The ethical is the universal. Moral laws or precepts, which are to be obeyed for their own sake, and not to serve any other end, or for any other motive, apply without exception to all human beings, who must obey them.

The sphere of the universal. See the ethical is the universal above.

The System. Hegel's philosophical system. See Context.

Theology. Setting out the beliefs and teachings of a religion in a systematic way; academic discipline concerned with the study of religion/religious beliefs and teachings.

Tillich. Paul Johannes (1886–1965). German-born theologian, philosopher and Lutheran minister. Professor at the University of Frankfurt and subsequently at the Harvard and Chicago Divinity Schools, his books include the three-volume *Systematic Theology, The Courage to Be* and *Dynamics of Faith*.

Tobias. The son of Tobit, who is sent on a debt-collecting mission by his father, and marries a widow, whose previous husbands have been killed, on their wedding-day, by an evil spirit. He drives out the evil spirit, by burning a fish's entrails.

Tragic hero. The central figure in a (series of) sad or solemn event(s), as in a Shakespearian tragedy.

Transparent. That which can be easily seen into, and about (the nature of) which there can be no mistake.

Under divine injunction. Subject to God's commands.

Universal. See the ethical is the universal above.

Unreflective happiness. Instinctive happiness, which has not been tested by careful reflection on the realities of life.

Validity. State of being sound, well-grounded.

Venerable. Entitled to respect on the basis of age or character.

Veritable clearance sale of ideas. What can rightly be called a selling-off of ideas at low prices.

Violate. Breach, disobey.

Virgin Mary. The mother of Jesus. See Luke 1.26–38.

Vocation. Calling, occupation or task to which someone feels called by God.

Wean. Get a baby used to food other than its mother's milk.

Glossary

Well-organized state. A well-governed state, subject to the rule of law, where existence is comfortable.

World of finitude. The ordinary world, where things are finite or limited.

World of spirit. The spiritual world, the divine world.